TELLING SECRETS

OTHER BOOKS BY FREDERICK BUECHNER

FICTION

A Long Day's Dying
The Seasons' Difference
The Return of Ansel Gibbs
The Final Beast
The Entrance to Porlock
Lion Country
Open Heart
Love Feast
Treasure Hunt
The Book of Bebb
Godric
Brendan
The Wizard's Tide

NONFICTION

The Magnificent Defeat
The Hungering Dark
The Alphabet of Grace
Wishful Thinking: A Theological ABC
The Faces of Jesus
Telling the Truth: The Gospel as Tragedy,
Comedy and Fairy Tale
Peculiar Treasures: A Biblical Who's Who
The Sacred Journey
Now and Then
A Room Called Remember
Whistling in the Dark

FREDERICK
BUECHNER *Telling*
Secrets

FREDERICK
BUECHNER *Telling*

Secrets

HarperSanFrancisco
A Division of HarperCollins*Publishers*

TELLING SECRETS. Copyright © 1991 by Frederick Buechner.
All rights reserved. Printed in the United States of America.
No part of this book may be used or reproduced in any manner
whatsoever without written permission except in the case
of brief quotations embodied in critical articles and reviews.
For information address HarperCollins Publishers,
10 East 53rd Street, New York, NY 10022.

FIRST EDITION

Library of Congress Cataloging-in-Publication Data

Buechner, Frederick.
   Telling secrets / Frederick Buechner—1st ed.
     p.   cm.
   ISBN 0–06–061181-2 (alk. paper)
   1. Buechner, Frederick. 2. Presbyterian Church—United
States—Clergy—Biography. I. Title.
BX9225.B768A3 1991
285′.1′092—dc20   90-41770
[B]   CIP

91 92 93 94 95 HAD 10 9 8 7 6 5 4 3 2 1

For Clayton Carlson

CONTENTS

INTRODUCTION

This is my third venture into autobiography, and I launch it on the world with the same misgivings as in the case of the earlier two. It is like telling somebody in detail how you are before they have asked the question, How are you? Indeed, it isn't like it; it *is* it. But I do it anyway because I need to do it. After forty years of writing books, I find I need to put things into words before I can believe that they are entirely real.

When it comes to putting my own life into words, however, the doubts persist even so. Are the events I describe anything like the way they really happened? As I look back over them, I think I see patterns, causal relationships, suggestions of meaning, that I was mostly unaware of at the time. Have I gotten them anything like right? E. M. Forster says that a story is a narrative of events arranged chronologically as in "the king died, and then the queen died," whereas a plot, although also a narrative of events, concentrates more on the *because* of things as in "the king died, and then the queen died of grief." This account is full of becauses. The question is, Have I actually discovered them, or, after long practice as a novelist, have I simply made them up? Have I concocted a plot out of what is only a story? Who knows? I can say only that to me life in general, including my life in particular, *feels* like a plot, and I find that a source both of strength and of fascination.

In *The Sacred Journey* and *Now and Then* I dealt mainly with the headlines of my life, like getting born, my father's early death, school, marriage, ordination, and so on. There are a few headlines in this book as well, but by and large it resembles more the back pages of the paper where I have always thought the real news is anyway—the reviews, an obituary or two, a couple of in-depth reports, the editorial and op-ed sections. It is the interior life especially that I have tried to deal with here because during the last fifteen years or so that this account covers I have found more and more that, like the back pages, it is in the interior where the real news is.

I have called this book *Telling Secrets* because I have come to believe that by and large the human family all has the same secrets, which are both very telling and very important to tell. They are telling in the sense that they tell what is perhaps the central paradox of our condition—that what we hunger for perhaps more than anything else is to be known in our full humanness, and yet that is often just what we also fear more than anything else. It is important to tell at least from time to time the secret of who we truly and fully are — even if we tell it only to ourselves — because otherwise we run the risk of losing track of who we truly and fully are and little by little come to accept instead the highly edited version which we put forth in hope that the world will find it more acceptable than the real thing. It is important to tell our secrets too because it makes it easier that way to see where we have been in our lives and where we are going. It also makes it easier for other people to tell us a secret or two of their own, and exchanges like that have a lot to do with what being a family is all about and what being human is all about. Finally, I suspect that it is by entering that deep place inside us where our secrets are kept that we come perhaps closer than we do anywhere else to the One who, whether we realize it or not, is of all our secrets the most telling and the most precious we have to tell.

ONE *The Dwarves in the Stable*

*O*NE November morning in 1936 when I was ten years old, my father got up early, put on a pair of gray slacks and a maroon sweater, opened the door to look in briefly on my younger brother and me, who were playing a game in our room, and then went down into the garage where he turned on the engine of the family Chevy and sat down on the running board to wait for the exhaust to kill him. Except for a memorial service for his Princeton class the next spring, by which time we had moved away to another part of the world altogether, there was no funeral because on both my mother's side and my father's there was no church connection of any kind and funerals were simply not part of the tradition. He was cremated, his ashes buried in a cemetery in Brooklyn, and I have no idea who if anybody was present. I know only that my mother, brother, and I were not.

There was no funeral to mark his death and put a period at the end of the sentence that had been his life, and as far as I can remember, once he had died my mother, brother, and I rarely talked about him much ever again, either to each other or to anybody else. It made my mother too sad to talk about him, and since there was already more than enough sadness to go round, my brother and I avoided the subject with her as she avoided it for her own reasons also with us. Once in a while she would bring it up but only in very oblique ways. I remember her saying things like "You're going to have to be big boys now," and "Now things are going to be different for all of us," and to me, "You're the man of the family now," with that one little three-letter adverb freighted with more grief and anger and guilt and God knows what all else than it could possibly bear.

We didn't talk about my father with each other, and we didn't talk about him outside the family either partly at least because suicide was looked on as something a little shabby and shameful in those days. Nice people weren't supposed to get mixed up with it. My father had tried to keep it a secret himself by leaving his note to my mother in a place where only she would be likely to find it and by saying a number of times the last few weeks of his life that there was something wrong with the Chevy's exhaust system, which he was going to see if he could fix. He did this partly in hopes that his life insurance wouldn't be invalidated, which of course it was, and partly too, I guess, in hopes that his friends wouldn't find out how he had died, which of course they did. His suicide was a secret we nonetheless tried to keep as best we could, and after a while my father himself became such a secret. There were times when he almost seemed a secret we were trying to keep from each other. I suppose there were occasions when one of us said, "Remember the time he did this," or, "Remember the time he said that," but if so, I've long since forgotten them. And because words are so much a part of what we keep the past alive by, if only words to ourselves, by not speaking of what we remembered about him we soon simply stopped remembering at all, or at least I did.

Within a couple of months of his death we moved away from New Jersey, where he had died, to the island of Bermuda of all places—another house, another country even—and from that point on I can't even remember remembering him. Within a year of his death I seem to have forgotten what he looked like except for certain photographs of him, to have forgotten what his voice sounded like and what it had been like to be with him. Because none of the three of us ever talked about how we had felt about him when he was alive or how we felt about him now that he wasn't, those feelings soon disappeared too and went underground along with the memories. As nearly as I can find out from people who knew him, he was a charming, good-looking, gentle man who was down on his luck and drank too much and had a great number of people who loved him and felt sorry for him. Among those people, however inadequately they may have showed it, I can only suppose were his wife and two sons; but in almost no time at all, it was as if, at least for me, he had never existed.

Don't talk, don't trust, don't feel is supposed to be the unwritten law of families that for one reason or another have gone out of whack, and certainly it was our law. We never talked about what had happened. We didn't trust the world with our secret, hardly even trusted each other with it. And as far as my ten-year-old self was concerned anyway, the only feeling I can remember from that distant time was the blessed relief of coming out of the dark and unmentionable sadness of my father's life and death into fragrance and greenness and light.

Don't talk, trust, feel was the law we lived by, and woe to the one who broke it. Twenty-two years later in a novel called *The Return of Ansel Gibbs* I told a very brief and fictionalized version of my father's death, and the most accurate word I can find to describe my mother's reaction to it is fury. For days she could hardly bring herself to speak to me, and when she did, it was with words of great bitterness. As she saw it, I had betrayed a sacred trust, and though I might have defended myself by saying that the story was after all as much mine as his son to tell as it was hers as his widow to keep hidden, I not only didn't say any such things but never even considered such things. I felt as much of a traitor as she charged me with being, and at the age of thirty-two was as horrified at what I had done as if I had been a child of ten. I was full of guilt and remorse and sure that in who-knows-what grim and lasting way I would be made to suffer for what I had done.

The Dwarves in the Stable

I was in my fifties and my mother in her eighties before I dared write on the forbidden subject again. It was in an autobiographical book called *The Sacred Journey* that I did so, and this time I told the story straight except that out of deference to her, or perhaps out of fear of her, I made no reference to her part in it. Otherwise I set it down as fully and accurately as I could, and the only reason I was able to do so was that I suspected that from *Ansel Gibbs* on my mother had never really read any other book I had written for fear of what she might find there. I was sure that she wouldn't read this one either. And I turned out to be right. She never read the book or the second autobiographical one that followed it even though, or precisely because, it was the story of her son's life and in that sense a part of her own story too. She was a strong and brave woman in many ways, but she was not brave and strong enough for that. We all have to survive as best we can.

She survived to within eleven days of her ninety-second birthday and died in her own bed in the room that for the last year or so of her life when her arthritic knees made it virtually impossible for her to walk became the only world that really interested her. She kept track more or less of the world outside. She had a rough idea what her children and grandchildren were up to. She read the papers and watched the evening news. But such things as that were dim and far away compared to the news that was breaking around her every day. Yvonne, who came days, had been trying to tell her something but God only knew what, her accent was so thick. Marge, who came nights, was an hour late because of delays on the subway, or so she said. My mother's cane had fallen behind the radiator, and the super was going to have to come do something about it. Where was her fan? Where was the gold purse she kept her extra hearing aids in? Where was the little peach-colored pillow, which of all the pillows she had was the only one that kept her tray level when they brought in her meals? In the world where she lived, these were the things that made headlines.

"If I didn't have something to look for, I would be lost," she said once. It was one of her most shimmering utterances. She hunted for her lost pills, lost handkerchief, lost silver comb, the little copy of *Les Malheurs de Sophie* she had lost, because with luck she might even find them. There was a better chance of it anyway than of finding her lost beauty or the friends who had mostly died or the life that had somehow gotten mislaid in the debris of her nonlife, all the aches and pains and indignities of having outlived almost everything including herself. But almost to the end she could laugh till the tears ran down and till our tears ran down. She loved telling how her father in the confusion of catching a train handed the red-cap his wallet once, or how one of her beaux had stepped through somebody's straw hat in the hall closet and was afraid to come out. Her laughter came from deep down in herself and deep down in the past, which in one way was lost and gone and in other ways was still as much within her reach as the can of root beer with a straw sticking in it which she always had on her bedside table because she said it was the only thing that helped her dry throat. The sad times she kept locked away never to be named, but the funny, happy times, the glamorous, romantic, young times, continued to be no less a part of her life than the furniture.

She excoriated the ravages of old age but never accepted them as the inevitable consequence of getting old. "I don't know what's wrong with me today," she must have said a thousand days as she tried once, then again, then a third time, to pull herself out of her chair into her walker. It never seemed to occur to her that what was wrong with her was that she was on her way to pushing a hundred. Maybe that was why some part of her remained unravaged. Some surviving lightness of touch let her stand back from the wreckage and see that among other things it was absurdly funny. When I told her the last time she was mobile enough to visit us in Vermont that the man who had just passed her window was the gardener, she said, "Tell him to come in and take a look at the last rose of summer."

She liked to paste gold stars on things or to antique things with gold paint — it was what she did with the past too of course — and lampshades, chairs, picture frames, tables, gleamed like treasure in the crazy little museum of her bedroom. The chaise longue was heaped with pillows, a fake leopard-skin throw, a velvet quilt, fashion magazines, movie magazines, catalogues stacked on a table beside it, stories by Dorothy Parker and Noel Coward, Kahlil Gibran's *The Prophet*. Victorian beadwork pincushions hung from the peach-colored walls along with pictures of happier times, greener places. The closet was a cotillion of pretty clothes she hadn't been able to wear for years, and her bureau overflowed with more of them—blouses, belts, costume jewelry, old evening purses, chiffon scarves, gloves. On top of the bureau stood perfume bottles, pill bottles, jars, tubes, boxes of patent medicine, a bowl of M & Ms, which she said were good for her. She had a theory that when you have a craving for something, including M & Ms, it means that your system needs it.

The living heart and command center of that room was the dressing table. When she was past getting out of her bed to sit at it any longer, what she needed from it was brought to her on a tray as soon as she woke up every morning, before breakfast even—the magnifying mirror, the lipsticks, eyebrow pencils, tweezers, face powder, hair brush, combs, cold cream, mascara. Before she did anything else, she did that and did it with such artistry that even within weeks of her end she managed a not implausible version of the face that since girlhood had been her principal fame and fairest fortune.

Over that dressing table there hung for years a mirror that I can remember from childhood. It was a mirror with an olive green wooden frame which she had once painted in oils with a little garland of flowers and medallions bearing the French words:

Il faut souffrir pour être belle. It was the motto of her life: You have to suffer in order to be beautiful. What she meant, of course, was all the pains she took in front of the mirror: the plucking and primping and powdering, the brushing and painting—that kind of suffering. But it seems clear that there was another kind too. To be born as blonde and blue-eyed and beautiful as she was can be as much of a handicap in its way as to be born with a cleft palate because if you are beautiful enough you don't really have to be anything much else to make people love you and want to be near you. You don't have to be particularly kind or unselfish or generous or compassionate because people will flock around you anyway simply for the sake of your *beaux yeux*. My mother could be all of those good things when she took a notion to, but she never made a habit of it. She never developed the giving, loving side of what she might have been as a human being, and, needless to say, that was where the real suffering came—the two failed marriages after the death of my father, the fact that among all the friends she had over the course of her life, she never as far as I know had one whom she would in any sense have sacrificed herself for and by doing so might perhaps have begun to find her best and truest self. W. B. Yeats in his poem "A Prayer for My Daughter" writes, "Hearts are not had as a gift but hearts are earned/By those that are not entirely beautiful." My almost entirely beautiful mother was by no means heartless, but I think hers was a heart that, who knows why, was rarely if ever touched in its deepest place. To let it be touched there was a risk that for reasons known only to her she was apparently not prepared to take.

For the twenty years or so she lived in New York she made no new friends because she chose to make none and lost all contact with the few old ones who were still alive. She believed in God, I think. With her eyes shut she would ask me what I thought about the afterlife from time to time, though when I tried to tell her she of course couldn't hear because it is hard to shout anything very much about the afterlife. But she never went to church. It always made her cry, she said. She wouldn't have been caught dead joining a club or group of any kind. "I know I'm queer," she often said. "I'm a very private person." And it was true. Even with the people closest to her she rarely spoke of what was going on inside her skin or asked that question of them. For the last fifteen years or so it reached the point where she saw virtually nobody except her immediate family and most of them not often. But by a miracle it didn't destroy her.

She had a cruel and terrible tongue when she was angry. When she struck, she struck to kill, and such killings must have been part of what she closed her eyes to, together with the other failures and mistakes of her life and the guilt they caused her, the shame she felt. But she never became bitter. She turned away from the world but never turned in upon herself. It was a kind of miracle, really. If she was lonely, I never heard her complain about it. Instead it was her looks she complained about: *My hair looks like straw. When I wake up in the morning I have this*

*awful red spot on my cheek. These God-awful teeth
don't fit. I don't know what's wrong with me today.*
From somewhere she was nourished, in other words,
and richly nourished, God only knows how, God only
knows. That was the other part of the miracle. Something deep within her stayed young, stayed beautiful
even, was never lost. And till the end of her life she
was as successful at not facing the reality of being a
very old woman as for almost a century she was successful at not facing her dark times as a young one.

Being beautiful was her business, her art, her delight, and it took her a long way and earned her many
dividends, but when, as she saw it, she lost her
beauty—you stand a better chance of finding your
cane behind the radiator than ever finding blue eyes
and golden hair again—she was like a millionaire
who runs out of money. She took her name out of the
phone book and got an unlisted number. She eventually became so deaf that it became almost impossible
to speak to her except about things simple enough to
shout—her health, the weather, when you would be
seeing her next. It was as if deafness was a technique
she mastered for not hearing anything that might
threaten her peace. She developed the habit of closing her eyes when she spoke to you as if you were a
dream she was dreaming. It was as if she chose not to
see in your face what you might be thinking behind
the simple words you were shouting, or as if, ostrich-
like, closing her eyes was a way of keeping you from
seeing her. With her looks gone she felt she had nothing left to offer the world, to propitiate the world. So

what she did was simply to check out of the world — that old, last rose of summer — the way Greta Garbo and Marlene Dietrich checked out of it, holing themselves up somewhere and never venturing forth except in disguise. My mother holed herself up in her apartment on 79th Street, then in just one room of that apartment, then in just one chair in that room, and finally in the bed where one morning a few summers ago, perhaps in her sleep, she died at last.

It is so easy to sum up other people's lives like this, and necessary too, of course, especially our parents' lives. It is a way of reducing their giant figures to a size we can manage, I suppose, a way of getting even maybe, of getting on, of saying goodbye. The day will come when somebody tries to sum you up the same way and also me. Tell me about old Buechner then. What was he really like? What made him tick? How did his story go? Well, you see, this happened and then that happened, and then that, and that is why he became thus and so, and why when all is said and done it is not so hard to understand why things turned out for him as they finally did. Is there any truth at all in the patterns we think we see, the explanations and insights that fall so readily from our tongues? Who knows. The main thing that leads me to believe that what I've said about my mother has at least a kind of partial truth is that I know at first hand that it is true of the mother who lives on in me and will always be part of who I am.

In the mid 1970s, as a father of three teenage children and a husband of some twenty years standing by

then, I would have said that my hearing was pretty good, that I could hear not only what my wife and children were saying but lots of things they weren't saying too. I would have said that I saw fairly well what was going on inside our house and what was going on inside me. I would also have said if anybody had asked me that our family was a close and happy one—that we had our troubles like everybody else but that we loved each other and respected each other and understood each other better than most. And in a hundred ways, praise God, I believe I was right. I believe that is the way it was. But in certain other ways, I came to learn, I was as deaf as my mother was with her little gold purse full of hearing aids none of which really ever worked very well, and though I did not shut my eyes when I talked to people the way she did, I shut them without knowing it to a whole dimension of the life that my wife and I and our children were living together on a green hillside in Vermont during those years.

There are two pieces of stained glass that sit propped up in one of the windows in the room where I write—a room paneled in old barn siding gone silvery gray with maybe as much as two centuries of weathering and full of a great many books, many of them considerably older than that which I've collected over the years and try to keep oiled and repaired because books are my passion, not only writing them and every once in a while even reading them but just having them and moving them around and feeling the comfort of their serene presence. One of those pieces of stained glass, which I think I asked somebody to give me one Christmas, shows the Cowardly Lion from *The Wizard of Oz* with his feet bound with rope and his face streaming with tears as a few of the Winged Monkeys who have bound him hover around in the background. The other is a diptych that somebody gave me once and that always causes me a twinge of embarrassment when I notice it because it seems a little too complacently religious. On one of its panels are written the words "May the blessing of God crown this house" and on the other "Fortunate is he whose work is blessed and whose household is prospered by the Lord."

I have never given either the lion or the diptych much thought as they've sat there year after year gathering dust, but I happened to notice them as I was preparing these pages and decided they might well serve as a kind of epigraph for this part of the story I'm telling. The Cowardly Lion is me, of course — crying, tied up, afraid. I am crying because at the time I'm speaking of, some fifteen years ago, a lot of sad and scary things were going on in our house that I felt helpless either to understand or to do anything about. Yet despite its rather self-satisfied religiosity, I believe the diptych is telling a truth about that time too.

I believe the blessing of God was indeed crowning our house in the sense that the sad and scary things themselves were, as it turned out, a fearsome blessing. And all the time those things were happening, the very fact that I was able to save my sanity by continuing to write among other things a novel called *Godric* made my work blessed and a means of grace at least for me. Nothing I've ever written came out of a darker time or brought me more light and comfort. It also—far more than I realized at the time I wrote it—brought me a sharper glimpse than I had ever had before of the crucial role my father has always played in my life and continues to play in my life even though in so many ways I have long since lost all but a handful of conscious memories of him.

I did not realize until after I wrote it how much of this there is in the book. When Godric is about to leave home to make his way in the world and his father Aedlward raises his hand to him in farewell, Godric says, "I believe my way went from that hand as a path goes from a door, and though many a mile that way has led me since, with many a turn and crossroad in between, if ever I should trace it back, it's to my father's hand that it would lead." And later, when he learns of his father's death, he says, "The sadness was I'd lost a father I had never fully found. It's like a tune that ends before you've heard it out. Your whole life through you search to catch the strain, and seek the face you've lost in strangers' faces." In writing passages like that, I was writing more than I had known I knew with the result that the book was not only a word *from* me—my words painstakingly chosen and arranged into sentences by me alone—but also a word out of such a deep and secret part of who I am that it seemed also a word *to* me.

If writers write not just with paper and ink or a word processor but with their own life's blood, then I think something like this is perhaps always the case. A book you write out of the depths of who you are, like a dream you dream out of those same depths, is entirely your own creation. All the words your characters speak are words that you alone have put into their mouths, just as every situation they become involved in is one that you alone have concocted for them. But it seems to me nonetheless that a book you write, like a dream you dream, can have more healing and truth and wisdom in it at least for yourself than you feel in any way responsible for.

A large part of the truth that *Godric* had for me was the truth that although death ended my father, it has never ended my relationship with my father—a secret that I had never so clearly understood before. So forty-four years after the last time I saw him, it was to my father that I dedicated the book—*In memoriam patris mei.* I wrote the dedication in Latin solely because at the time it seemed appropriate to the medieval nature of the tale, but I have come to suspect since that Latin was also my unconscious way of remaining obedient to the ancient family law that the secret of my father must be at all costs kept secret.

The other half of the diptych's message—"whose household is prospered by the Lord"—was full of irony. Whether because of the Lord or good luck or the state of the stock market, we were a prosperous family in more ways than just economic, but for all the good our prosperity did us when the chips were down, we might as well have been paupers.

The Dwarves in the Stable

What happened was that one of our daughters began to stop eating. There was nothing scary about it at first. It was just the sort of thing any girl who thought she'd be prettier if she lost a few pounds might do—nothing for breakfast, maybe a carrot or a Diet Coke for lunch, for supper perhaps a little salad with low calorie dressing. But then, as months went by, it did become scary. Anorexia nervosa is the name of the sickness she was suffering from, needless to say, and the best understanding of it that I have been able to arrive at goes something like this. Young people crave to be free and independent. They crave also to be taken care of and safe. The dark magic of anorexia is that it satisfies both of these cravings at once. By not eating, you take your stand against the world that is telling you what to do and who to be. And by not eating you also make your body so much smaller, lighter, weaker that in effect it becomes a child's body again and the world flocks to your rescue. This double victory is so great that apparently not even self-destruction seems too high a price to pay.

Be that as it may, she got more and more thin, of course, till she began to have the skull-like face and fleshless arms and legs of a victim of Buchenwald, and at the same time the Cowardly Lion got more and more afraid and sad, felt more and more helpless. No rational argument, no dire medical warning, no pleading or cajolery or bribery would make this young woman he loved eat normally again but only seemed to strengthen her determination not to, this young woman on whose life his own in so many ways depended. He could not solve her problem because he was of course himself part of her problem. She remained very much the same person she had always been—creative, loving, funny, bright as a star—but she was more afraid of gaining weight than she was afraid of death itself because that was what it came to finally. Three years were about as long as the sickness lasted in its most intense form with some moments when it looked as though things were getting better and some moments when it was hard to imagine they could get any worse. Then finally, when she had to be hospitalized, a doctor called one morning to say that unless they started feeding her against her will, she would die. It was as clear-cut as that. Tears ran down the Cowardly Lion's face as he stood with the telephone at his ear. His paws were tied. The bat-winged monkeys hovered.

I will not try to tell my daughter's story for two reasons. One is that it is not mine to tell but hers. The other is that of course I do not know her story, not the real story, the inside story, of what it was like for her. For the same reasons I will not try to tell what it was like for my wife or our other two children, each of whom in her own way was involved in that story. I can tell only my part in it, what happened to me, and even there I can't be sure I have it right because in many ways it is happening still. The fearsome blessing of that hard time continues to work itself out in my life in the same way we're told the universe is still hurtling through outer space under the impact of the great cosmic explosion that brought it into being in the first place. I think grace sometimes explodes into our lives like that — sending our pain, terror, astonishment hurtling through inner space until by grace they become Orion, Cassiopeia, Polaris to give us our bearings, to bring us into something like full being at last.

My anorectic daughter was in danger of starving to death, and without knowing it, so was I. I wasn't living my own life any more because I was so caught up in hers. If in refusing to eat she was mad as a hatter, I was if anything madder still because whereas in some sense she knew what she was doing to herself, I knew nothing at all about what I was doing to myself. She had given up food. I had virtually given up doing anything in the way of feeding myself humanly. To be at peace is to have peace inside yourself more or less in spite of what is going on outside yourself. In that sense I had no peace at all. If on one particular day she took it into her head to have a slice of toast, say, with her dietetic supper, I was in seventh heaven. If on some other day she decided to have no supper at all, I was in hell.

I choose the term *hell* with some care. Hell is where there is no light but only darkness, and I was so caught up in my fear for her life, which had become in a way my life too, that none of the usual sources of light worked any more, and light was what I was starving for. I had the companionship of my wife and two other children. I read books. I played tennis and walked in the woods. I saw friends and went to the movies. But even in the midst of such times as that I remained so locked inside myself that I was not really present in them at all. Toward the end of C. S. Lewis's *The Last Battle* there is a scene where a group of dwarves sit huddled together in a tight little knot thinking that they are in a pitch black, malodorous stable when the truth of it is that they are out in the midst of an endless grassy countryside as green as Vermont with the sun shining and blue sky overhead. The huge golden lion, Aslan himself, stands nearby with all the other dwarves "kneeling in a circle around his forepaws" as Lewis writes, "and burying their hands and faces in his mane as he stooped his great head to touch them with his tongue." When Aslan offers the dwarves food, they think it is offal. When he offers them wine, they take it for ditch water. "Perfect love casteth out fear," John writes (1 John 4:18), and the other side of that is that fear like mine casteth out love, even God's love. The love I had for my daughter was lost in the anxiety I had for my daughter.

The only way I knew to be a father was to take care of her, as my father had been unable to take care of me, to move heaven and earth if necessary to make her well, and of course I couldn't do that. I didn't have either the wisdom or the power to make her well. None of us has the power to change other human beings like that, and it would be a terrible power if we did, the power to violate the humanity of others even for their own good. The psychiatrists we consulted told me I couldn't cure her. The best thing I could do for her was to stop trying to do anything. I think in my heart I knew they were right, but it didn't stop the madness of my desperate meddling, it didn't stop the madness of my trying. Everything I could think to do or say only stiffened her resolve to be free from, among other things, me. Her not eating was a symbolic way of striking out for that freedom. The only way she would ever be well again was if and when she freely chose to be. The best I could do as her father was to stand back and give her that freedom even at the risk of her using it to choose for death instead of life.

Love your neighbor as yourself is part of the great commandment. The other way to say it is, Love yourself as your neighbor. Love yourself not in some egocentric, self-serving sense but love yourself the way you would love your friend in the sense of taking care of yourself, nourishing yourself, trying to understand, comfort, strengthen yourself. Ministers in particular, people in the caring professions in general, are famous for neglecting their selves with the result that they are apt to become in their own way as helpless and crippled as the people they are trying to care for and thus no longer selves who can be of much use to anybody. If your daughter is struggling for life in a raging torrent, you do not save her by jumping into the torrent with her, which leads only to your both drowning together. Instead you keep your feet on the dry bank—you maintain as best you can your own inner peace, the best and strongest of who you are— and from that solid ground reach out a rescuing hand. "Mind your own business" means butt out of other people's lives because in the long run they must live their lives for themselves, but it also means pay mind to your own life, your own health and wholeness, both for your own sake and ultimately for the sake of those you love too. Take care of yourself so you can take care of them. A bleeding heart is of no help to anybody if it bleeds to death.

How easy it is to write such words and how impossible it was to live them. What saved the day for my daughter was that when she finally had to be hospitalized in order to keep her alive, it happened about three thousand miles away from me. I was not there to protect her, to make her decisions, to manipulate events on her behalf, and the result was that she had to face those events on her own. There was no one to shield her from those events and their consequences in all their inexorability. In the form of doctors, nurses, social workers, the judge who determined that she was a danger to her own life and thus could be legally hospitalized against her will, society stepped in. Those men and women were not haggard, dithering, lovesick as I was. They were realistic, tough, conscientious, and in those ways, though they would never have put it in such terms themselves, loved her in a sense that I believe is closer to what Jesus meant by love than what I had been doing.

God loves in something like their way, I think. The power that created the universe and spun the dragonfly's wing and is beyond all other powers holds back, in love, from overpowering us. I have never felt God's presence more strongly than when my wife and I visited that distant hospital where our daughter was. Walking down the corridor to the room that had her name taped to the door, I felt that presence surrounding me like air—God in his very stillness, holding his breath, loving her, loving us all, the only way he can without destroying us. One night we went to compline in an Episcopal cathedral, and in the coolness and near emptiness of that great vaulted place, in the remoteness of the choir's voices chanting plainsong, in the grayness of the stone, I felt it again—the passionate restraint and hush of God.

Little by little the young woman I loved began to get well, emerging out of the shadows finally as strong and sane and wise as anybody I know, and little by little as I watched her healing happen, I began to see how much I was in need of healing and getting well myself. Like Lewis's dwarves, for a long time I had sat huddled in the dark of a stable of my own making. It was only now that I started to suspect the presence of the green countryside, the golden lion in whose image and likeness even cowardly lions are made.

This is all part of the story about what it has been like for the last ten years or so to be me, and before anybody else has the chance to ask it, I will ask it myself: Who cares? What in the world could be less important than who I am and who my father and mother were, the mistakes I have made together with the occasional discoveries, the bad times and good times, the moments of grace. If I were a public figure and my story had had some impact on the world at large, that might be some justification for telling it, but I am a very private figure indeed, living very much out of the mainstream of things in the hills of Vermont, and my life has had very little impact on anybody much except for the people closest to me and the comparative few who have read books I've written and been one way or another touched by them.

But I talk about my life anyway because if, on the one hand, hardly anything could be less important, on the other hand, hardly anything could be more important. My story is important not because it is mine, God knows, but because if I tell it anything like right, the chances are you will recognize that in many ways it is also yours. Maybe nothing is more important than that we keep track, you and I, of these stories of who we are and where we have come from and the people we have met along the way because it is precisely through these stories in all their particularity, as I have long believed and often said, that God makes himself known to each of us most powerfully and personally. If this is true, it means that to lose track of our stories is to be profoundly impoverished not only humanly but also spiritually.

The God of biblical faith is a God who started history going in the first place. He is also a God who moment by moment, day by day continues to act in history always, which means both the history that gets written down in the *New York Times* and the *San Francisco Chronicle* and at the same time my history and your history, which for the most part don't get written down anywhere except in the few lines that may be allotted to us some day on the obituary page. The Exodus, the Covenant, the entry into the Promised

Land—such mighty acts of God as these appear in
Scripture, but no less mighty are the acts of God as
they appear in our own lives. I think of my father's
death as in its way his exodus, his escape from bond-
age, and of the covenant that my mother made with
my brother and me never to talk about him, and of the
promised land of pre–World War II Bermuda that we
reached through the wilderness and bewilderness of
our first shock and grief at losing him.

As I understand it, to say that God is mightily
present even in such private events as these does not
mean that he makes events happen to us which move
us in certain directions like chessmen. Instead, events
happen under their own steam as random as rain,
which means that God is present in them not as their
cause but as the one who even in the hardest and most
hair-raising of them offers us the possibility of that
new life and healing which I believe is what salvation
is. For instance I cannot believe that a God of love and
mercy in any sense willed my father's suicide; it was
my father himself who willed it as the only way out
available to him from a life that for various reasons
he had come to find unbearable. God did not will
what happened that early November morning in
Essex Fells, New Jersey, but I believe that God was
present in what happened. I cannot guess how he was
present with my father—I can guess much better how
utterly abandoned by God my father must have felt if
he thought about God at all—but my faith as well as
my prayer is that he was and continues to be present
with him in ways beyond my guessing. I can speak

with some assurance only of how God was present in that dark time for me in the sense that I was not destroyed by it but came out of it with scars that I bear to this day, to be sure, but also somehow the wiser and the stronger for it. Who knows how I might have turned out if my father had lived, but through the loss of him all those long years ago I think that I learned something about how even tragedy can be a means of grace that I might never have come to any other way. As I see it, in other words, God acts in history and in your and my brief histories not as the puppeteer who sets the scene and works the strings but rather as the great director who no matter what role fate casts us in conveys to us somehow from the wings, if we have our eyes, ears, hearts open and sometimes even if we don't, how we can play those roles in a way to enrich and ennoble and hallow the whole vast drama of things including our own small but crucial parts in it.

In fact I am inclined to believe that God's chief purpose in giving us memory is to enable us to go back in time so that if we didn't play those roles right the first time round, we can still have another go at it now. We cannot undo our old mistakes or their consequences any more than we can erase old wounds that we have both suffered and inflicted, but through the power that memory gives us of thinking, feeling, imagining our way back through time we can at long last finally finish with the past in the sense of removing its power to hurt us and other people and to stunt our growth as human beings.

The sad things that happened long ago will always remain part of who we are just as the glad and gracious things will too, but instead of being a burden of guilt, recrimination, and regret that make us constantly stumble as we go, even the saddest things can become, once we have made peace with them, a source of wisdom and strength for the journey that still lies ahead. It is through memory that we are able to reclaim much of our lives that we have long since written off by finding that in everything that has happened to us over the years God was offering us possibilities of new life and healing which, though we may have missed them at the time, we can still choose and be brought to life by and healed by all these years later.

Another way of saying it, perhaps, is that memory makes it possible for us both to bless the past, even those parts of it that we have always felt cursed by, and also to be blessed by it. If this kind of remembering sounds like what psychotherapy is all about, it is because of course it is, but I think it is also what the forgiveness of sins is all about—the interplay of God's forgiveness of us and our forgiveness of God and each other. To see how God's mercy was for me buried deep even in my father's death was not just to be able to forgive my father for dying and God for letting him die so young and without hope and all the people like my mother who were involved in his death but also to be able to forgive myself for all the years I had failed to air my crippling secret so that then, however slowly and uncertainly, I could start to find healing. It is in the experience of such healing that I believe we experience also God's loving forgiveness of us, and insofar as memory is the doorway to both experiences, it becomes not just therapeutic but sacred.

In a book called *The Wizard's Tide* I wrote the story of my father's death the way I would tell it to a child, in other words the way I need to tell it to the child who lives on inside me as the children we were live on inside all of us. By telling it as a story, I told it not from the outside as an observer, the way I have told it in these pages, but from the inside as a participant. By telling it in language a child could understand, I told it as the child who I both was in 1936 and still am in 1990. I relived it for that child and *as* that child with the difference that this time I was able to live it right.

The father in the story dies in much the way my father did, and the mother and the children in the story hushed it up in much the way my mother and her two children did, but then comes the difference. At the end of the story, on Christmas eve, the boy Teddy, who is me, comes to a momentous conclusion. "He thought about how terrible it was that nobody talked about [his father] any more so that it was almost as if there had never been any such person. He decided that from now on he wanted to talk about him a lot. He wanted to remember everything about him that he could remember so someday he could tell about him to other people who had never seen him." And then, just before turning off the lights, Teddy actually does this. For the first time since his father's death, Teddy brings the subject up to his younger sister, Bean. He doesn't say anything about his father, he just mentions his name, but as I wrote the story, I knew that was enough. It was enough to start a healing process for the children in the story that for me didn't start till I was well into my fifties. Stranger still, it was enough also to start healing the child in me the way he might have been healed in 1936 if his real story had only turned out like the make-believe story in the book. By a kind of miracle, the make-believe story *became* the real story or vice versa. The unalterable past was in some extraordinary way altered. Maybe the most sacred function of memory is just that: to render the distinction between past, present, and future ultimately meaningless; to enable us at some level of our being to inhabit that same eternity which it is said that God himself inhabits.

We believe in God—such as it is, we have faith—because certain things happened to us once and go on happening. We work and goof off, we love and dream, we have wonderful times and awful times, are cruelly hurt and hurt others cruelly, get mad and bored and scared stiff and ache with desire, do all such human things as these, and if our faith is not mainly just window dressing or a rabbit's foot or fire insurance, it is because it grows out of precisely this kind of rich human compost. The God of biblical faith is the God who meets us at those moments in which for better or worse we are being most human, most ourselves, and if we lose touch with those moments, if we don't stop from time to time to notice what is happening to us and around us and inside us, we run the tragic risk of losing touch with God too.

Sad to say, the people who seem to lose touch with themselves and with God most conspicuously are of all things ministers. As a minister myself I am peculiarly aware of this. I don't say they do it more than other people but they do it more publicly. It could hardly be more ironic. First of all, ministers give preeminence to of all books the Bible whose absolutely central and unifying thesis is that God makes himself known in historical experience. Secondly, they call their congregations to examine their own experience as human beings in that most intimate and searching of all ways which is known as prayer. Thirdly, in their sermons, if they do it right, they proclaim above all else the staggeringly good news that God so loves the world that he is continually at work in our lives in the world in order to draw us, in love, closer and closer to himself and to each other. In other words, a major part of their ministry is to remind us that there is nothing more important than to pay attention to what is happening to us, yet again and again they show little sign of doing so themselves. There is precious little in most of their preaching to suggest that they have rejoiced and suffered with the rest of mankind. If they draw on their own experience at all, it is usually for some little anecdote to illustrate a point or help make the pill go down but rarely if ever for an authentic, first-hand, flesh-and-blood account of what it is like to love Christ, say, or to feel spiritually bankrupt, or to get fed up with the whole religious enterprise.

Along with much of the rest of mankind, ministers have had such moments, we can only assume, but more often than not they don't seem to trust them, don't draw on them, don't talk about them. Instead they keep setting them aside for some reason—maybe because they seem too private to share or too trivial or too ambiguous or not religious enough; maybe because what God seems to be saying to them through their flesh-and-blood experience has a depth and mystery and power to it which make all their homiletical pronouncements about God sound empty by comparison. The temptation then is to stick to the homiletical pronouncements. Comparatively empty as they may be, they are at least familiar. They add up. Congregations have come to expect homiletical pronouncements and to take comfort from them, and the preachers who pronounce them can move them around in various thought-provoking and edifying ways which nobody will feel unsettled or intimidated by because they have heard them so often.

Ministers run the awful risk, in other words, of ceasing to be witnesses to the presence in their own lives—let alone in the lives of the people they are trying to minister to—of a living God who transcends everything they think they know and can say about him and is full of extraordinary surprises. Instead they tend to become *professionals* who have mastered all the techniques of institutional religion and who speak on religious matters with what often seems a maximum of authority and a minimum of vital personal involvement. Their sermons often sound as

bland as they sound bloodless. The faith they proclaim appears to be no longer rooted in or nourished
by or challenged by their own lives but instead free-
floating, secondhand, passionless. They sound, in
other words, burnt out.

Obviously ministers are not called to be in that
sense professionals. God forbid. I believe that they are
called instead, together with all other Christians and
would-be Christians, to consider the lilies of the field,
to consider the least of these my brethren, to consider
the dead sparrow by the roadside. Maybe prerequisite
to all those, they are called upon to consider themselves — what they love and what they fear, what they
are ashamed of, what makes them sick to their stom-
achs, what rejoices their hearts. I believe that ministers and everyone are called also to consider Jesus of
Nazareth in whom God himself showed how crucial
human life is by actually living one and hallowed
human death by actually dying one and who lives
and dies still with us and for us and in spite of us. I believe that we are called to see that the day-by-day lives
of all of us — the things that happened long ago, the
things that happened only this morning — are also
hallowed and crucial and part of a great drama in which
souls are lost and souls are saved including our own.

That is why to keep track of these lives we live is
not just a means of enriching our understanding and
possibly improving our sermons but a truly sacred
work. In these pages I tell secrets about my parents,
my children, myself because that is one way of keeping track and because I believe that it is not only more

honest but also vastly more interesting than to pretend that I have no such secrets to tell. I not only have my secrets, I am my secrets. And you are your secrets. Our secrets are human secrets, and our trusting each other enough to share them with each other has much to do with the secret of what it is to be human.

TWO **The White Tower**

"*T*HEN God said, 'Let us make man in our image, after our likeness, and let them have dominion over the fish of the sea, and over the birds of the air, and over the cattle, and over all the earth, and over every creeping thing that creeps upon the earth.' So God created man in his own image, in the image of God he created him; male and female he created them." (Gen. 1:26–27)

Who knows what I have in me of the deaf old lady on 79th Street and the young man in gray slacks and a maroon sweater who in their heyday begot me? Who knows what all of us have in us not just of our parents but of their parents before them and so on back beyond any names we know or any faces we would recognize if we came upon their portraits hanging on an antique shop wall? Who knows what we carry in us either from those unspeaking, unthinking creatures that slithered and crept their way through the millennia until they turned into the likes of you and me and who have never stopped speaking and thinking since? And you can carry it back farther even than that to whatever unimaginable event took place in one instant of time to bring time itself into being, and space itself, and that basic matter of which you and I and the star Aldebaran and the tooth of the great white shark and the petal of the rose are all composed. As individuals, as a species, as a world, our origins are lost in mystery.

The passage from Genesis points to a mystery greater still. It says that we come from farther away then space and longer ago than time. It says that evolution and genetics and environment explain a lot about us but they don't explain all about us or even the most important thing about us. It says that though we live in the world, we can never be entirely at home in the world. It says in short not only that we were created by God but also that we were created in God's image and likeness. We have something of God within us the way we have something of the stars.

Life batters and shapes us in all sorts of ways before it's done, but those original selves which we were born with and which I believe we continue in some measure to be no matter what are selves which still echo with the holiness of their origin. I believe that what Genesis suggests is that this original self, with the print of God's thumb still upon it, is the most essential part of who we are and is buried deep in all of us as a source of wisdom and strength and healing which we can draw upon or, with our terrible freedom, not draw upon as we choose. I think that among other things all real art comes from that deepest self—painting, writing music, dance, all of it that in some way nourishes the spirit and enriches the understanding. I think that our truest prayers come from there too, the often unspoken, unbidden prayers that can rise out of the lives of unbelievers as well as believers whether they recognize them as prayers or not. And I think that from there also come our best dreams and our times of gladdest playing and taking it easy and all those moments when we find ourselves being better or stronger or braver or wiser than we are.

This is the self we are born with, and then of course the world does its work. Starting with the rather too pretty young woman, say, and the charming but rather unstable young man who together know no more about being parents than they do about the far side of the moon, the world sets in to making us into what the world would like us to be, and because we have to survive after all, we try to make ourselves into something that we hope the world will like better than it apparently did the selves we originally were. That is the story of all our lives, needless to say, and in the process of living out that story, the original, shimmering self gets buried so deep that most of us end up hardly living out of it at all. Instead we live out all the other selves which we are constantly putting on and taking off like coats and hats against the world's weather.

I think here of the Tower of London. More particularly I think of that oldest part of it, known as the White Tower, which was built by William the Conqueror in the eleventh century. On the second floor of

it there is a small Norman chapel called the Chapel of
Saint John. It is very bare and very simple. It is built
all of stone with twelve stone pillars and a vaulted
ceiling. There is a cool, silvery light that comes in
through the arched windows. Knights of the Order of
the Bath used to keep all-night vigil there over their
armor before being anointed by the king on his coronation day. The chapel is very silent, very still. It is
almost a thousand years old. You cannot enter it without being struck by the feeling of purity and peace it
gives. If there is any such thing in the world, it is a
holy place.

But that is not all there is in the White Tower.
Directly below the chapel is the most terrible of all
the tower's dungeons. It has a heavy oak door that
locks out all light and ventilation. It measures only
four feet square by four feet high so that a prisoner has
no way either to stand upright in it or to lie down at
full length. There is almost no air to breathe in it, almost no room to move. It is known as the Little Ease.

I am the White Tower of course. To one degree or
another all of us are. During the time of my daughter's
sickness and its aftermath I began to realize how
much of my time I spent in that dark, airless, crippling place where there was no ease at all. I began to
understand that though in many ways we were both a
lucky and loving family, my daughter's anorexia was
only the most visible manifestation of a complex,
subterranean malaise that we were all five of us suffering from — myself maybe most of all. The craving to be
free and independent on the one hand and to be taken

care of and safe on the other were as much mine as they were my daughter's. Beneath the question about food, there were for her unspoken questions about love, trust, fear, loss, separation, and these were also my questions. Childhood fears persist in us all, and what I feared most was losing what I loved the way years before I had lost a father I hardly knew well enough to love. So I clung onto my children for dear life because in many ways, too many ways, they were my life. I looked to them and to my wife to fill empty places in me which, with their own lives to live, they didn't have either the wherewithal or the inclination to do. I got so caught up in my daughter's slow starvation that I wasn't aware of the extent to which I myself was starving.

Life went on of course because that is what life does. I kept on writing books, which a relatively small but faithful audience kept on reading. It was at this time that I wrote two short autobiographical volumes called *The Sacred Journey* in 1982 and *Now and Then* in 1983, and they helped let a little light and air into the dark place where I was imprisoned. They gave me more of a sense than I had ever had before of how as far back as I could remember things had been stirring in my life that I was all but totally unaware of at the time. If anybody had predicted when I was an undergraduate at Princeton that I was going to be ordained as a minister ten years after graduation, I think I would have been flabbergasted. Yet as I wrote those two autobiographical volumes I found myself remembering small events as far back as early childhood which were even then leading me in something like that direction but so subtly and almost imperceptibly that it wasn't until decades had passed that I saw them for what they were — or thought I did because you can never be sure whether you are discovering that kind of truth or inventing it. The events were often so small that I was surprised to remember them, yet they turned out to have been road markers on a journey I didn't even know I was taking. The people involved in them were often people I had never thought of as having played particularly significant roles in my life yet looking back at them I saw that, for me, they had been life-givers, saints.

I wrote, for instance, about a nurse my brother and I had had when we were little boys in Washington, D.C., who had false teeth which she could make drop at will to our delectation and who taught us to sing "The Old Rugged Cross" in our beds at night before either of us had any idea, as I put it, what a hymn was or what a cross was or why it was something to sing about in the dark. I wrote too about a minister who shortly after my first novel was published in 1950 asked me out of the blue if I had ever considered putting my talents to work for Christ, and I remember cringing with embarrassment at that kind of language and thinking he must have gone out of his mind.

I also described what from the outside looked like a trivial domestic scene with my mother but which turned out to be such a watershed of my life that I must describe it briefly now. We were just about to have a pleasant dinner together when a friend of mine telephoned to say that his family had been in an awful accident and to ask if I would come wait with him at the airport where he was to catch a plane to where the accident had happened. My mother was furious. She said I was a fool to think of ruining our evening together for such a ridiculous reason as that, and for a moment I was horrified to find myself thinking that maybe she was right. Then the next moment I saw more clearly than I ever had before that it is on just such outwardly trivial decisions as this—should I go or should I stay—that human souls are saved or lost. I also saw for what was maybe the first time in my life that we are called to love our neighbors not just for our neighbors' sake but for our own sake, and that when John wrote, "He who does not love remains in death" (1 John 3:14), he was stating a fact of nature as incontrovertible as gravity. And even as I was writing about moments like that in those two books, the same kind of moments kept on happening.

For instance, I remember sitting parked by the roadside once, terribly depressed and afraid about my daughter's illness and what was going on in our family, when out of nowhere a car came along down the highway with a license plate that bore on it the one word out of all the words in the dictionary that I needed most to see exactly then. The word was TRUST. What do you call a moment like that? Something to laugh off as the kind of joke life plays on us every once in a while? The word of God? I am willing to believe that maybe it was something of both, but for me it was an epiphany. The owner of the car turned out to be, as I'd suspected, a trust officer in a bank, and not long ago, having read an account I wrote of the incident somewhere, he found out where I lived and one afternoon brought me the license plate itself, which sits propped up on a bookshelf in my house to this day. It is rusty around the edges and a little battered, and it is also as holy a relic as I have ever seen.

Another gift that turned up in those dark days was a new great friend. I was inclined to believe that by the time you hit your fifties, the moment for making great friends has passed. I was wrong. His name was Dudley Ian Caithness Knott, an Englishman who had been at various times a naval officer during the Second World War, a filmmaker, a publisher, and an executive in British Petroleum. When I met him, soon after a nearly fatal bout with lung cancer, he was simply keeping as richly alive as he could manage under the circumstances with the help of his richly alive Charlestonian wife, Katty. I didn't speak to him about my troubles much any more than as an Englishman who held such cards as that pretty close to his chest he spoke to me much about his; but in spite of that, or because of that, I found great healing in the continual astonishment and delight of knowing him. That deadpan, owlish, English face under the visor of the Greek fisherman's cap that he perpetually wore; his tales of Nanny Bampton—"No, no, Master Dudley, you mustn't touch little Mildred *there*"; the way he might at any moment bellow out, in his stentorian off-key baritone, some scrap of music hall ribaldry—"Put your belly next to mine and wiggle your bum"—or other

sonorities that caught his fancy, such as "James and John the sons of Zebedee" or the single name "Zimbabwe!" shouted out like a battle cry; the rubber Snoopy doll that traveled with him wherever he went marked on its chest with where, on his own chest, they had tried to burn away his cancer with radiation. I never knew what he would do next or say next, but I was never in any doubt as to who he was, which was, for me, a human being I could talk to about almost anything, somebody I could be as much myself with as I am capable of being with almost anybody. On certain occasions — like seeing his sheer ecstasy as our dachshund Rätsel made one of his running dives eight feet out into the middle of a swimming pool — I laughed with Dudley Knott laughter that had such self-forgetfulness and friendship and gladness in it that it was a kind of holy communion of laughter.

But for all those good things that happened, the Little Ease was where I spent much of those years. It is hard to see how I could have survived the worst of that time without the sense of God's presence in my life in just such ways as I have been describing, and in books I have read for the first time, like Mary Strong's *Letters of the Scattered Brotherhood*, and others I read again like Thomas Kelly's *A Testament of Devotion*, and in the prayers I continually and clumsily prayed because there seemed to be some voice in me that couldn't stop praying them, and in friends like Dudley. But the one place where I did not look to find God's presence because I'm not sure I even knew such a place existed was that Chapel of Saint John within

us all where the deepest truth of who we are keeps
vigil, that still, silent place where there is forgiveness
and healing and hope. Indeed, the best way I can find
to describe my life from the time when those family
troubles began some twelve years ago until now is as
a series of bumbling, myopic, famished attempts to
find the peace of that ancient and holy place which,
together with the dungeon of the Little Ease, I believe
is part of the White Tower that all of us are.

After being discharged from the hospital, our
anorectic daughter came home to Vermont where little by little she began to pick up her life again. She
started to eat again — not much at first to be sure and
bizarre kinds of food eaten at bizarre times and in bizarre ways, but enough to keep her going anyway and
to start making her look gradually less hollow-eyed,
hollow-cheeked, skeletal. When I first saw her in the
hospital I wouldn't have recognized her as my daughter if I hadn't known. She saw a psychotherapist regu-
larly. She entered a 12-step program, which more
than anything else, she says, saved her life. She made
new friends. She went back to college, and by the
time she graduated in 1983, even I could at last believe that she was probably going to be well again.
Since then she has emerged from her brush with
madness and death into health and wholeness that I
marvel at. It need not have turned out that way, it
nearly did not turn out that way, but it did turn out
that way. And then, and then — ironically or provi-
dentially — it was her increasing wellness that made
me realize that in many ways I was not well. I would

have thought that now at last with her on her way
back to health I could draw a healthy breath again myself, but in that four-foot cube of darkness behind the
heavy door there is hardly any air to breathe, hardly
any room to move.

I tried psychotherapy myself—the same therapist
who had helped me through the worst of my daughter's illness—but one incident can stand for more or
less the whole experience. During one of our sessions
I had the feeling that the therapist was trying to lead
me to some major insight that might help save the day
for me. When I asked if that was the case, she acknowl-
edged it, but when I asked if she would be willing
simply to tell me in so many words what the insight
was, she demurred. That was not the way psychotherapy worked, she said. It was something I would have
to come to on my own if it was to have any real value
for me, she said, or something like that. But then as
the end of the hour drew near, she relented and put
into words what it was she had been trying to lead me
to see. There was nothing in the world just then that I
was more fascinated to hear—for all I knew my recov-
ery itself might depend on it—but even later that same
day I couldn't have told you what she said nor could I
possibly tell you now. I was simply not ready to hear
it yet. The words I could hear all right, but in terms of
their meaning I was as deaf as my mother before me
and possibly, like her, because I chose to be deaf. Possibly I was not ready to be well yet either. The Little
Ease is a place of torment, but if you live there long
enough, it eventually becomes home. If you manage

to escape it, where do you go next, who do you become next? If after all those years you get well, what do you do with your wellness? The responsibility is staggering. The freedom is staggering.

Picture a white house near the road on a green Vermont hillside. The house looks east down across a pasture where there are usually a few horses grazing, a pasture pond. Across the road there is more pasture sloping steeply up to where there used to be a tree we called the flying birch because after years of doing battle with the high winds up there it was so bent and ravaged that it looked as if it was about to take off into the wind. Except for two other houses nearby, there is no further sign of human habitation as far as the eye can see — just the near hills, the farther hills, and then the farthest, green in summer, mauve in winter, and in the autumn, when the leaves turn, a conflagration that must be seen to be believed.

It is Paradise, of course, and so in a way is the white house. There is nothing fancy about it — just a number of small bedrooms, a small narrow living room looking down toward the pond and the horses, and the good-sized room we built on when the children were little so there would be a place to get away from the hurly burly of things, the room paneled with weathered barn boards where the Cowardly Lion weeps stained glass tears and the rather too smugly religious diptych says "Fortunate is he whose work is blessed" and where I mostly do what I always feel a little uncomfortable about calling work because there is so much about it that feels instead like a kind of play. That room is filled with books, and the rest of the house is full too after some twenty-five years of living in it—full of other books, full of the children's toys, stuffed animals, records, pictures, the back porch full of my wife's gardening paraphernalia, of bridles and harnesses waiting to be cleaned, full of coats and boots for bad weather.

As the children started leaving home for lives of their own, they left their empty rooms behind so that emptiness is another of the things the house became full of, beds rarely slept in any more, closet doors rarely opened. Any fool knows that when you have children, your whole life changes, but I was a fool who never realized the extent to which when you have your children no longer, your life changes again and almost more radically. Somebody who writes books spends hours alone, and in the days when the children were there to come back from school, they brought the world back with them. They brought tales of their adventures back with them to me whose only adventures most days had taken place inside my head. As surely as they brought back homework, they brought back home to that house, brought back more than anything else themselves to that house. And if they didn't come back when I expected them to, especially at night, I would stand at the window trying to suck out of the dungeon darkness with my eyes the sight of their headlights winding up the long hill or I would lie in my bed thinking that no silence so heavy and smothering could ever draw apart enough to let through the blessed sound of their car pulling up by the stone wall, the flip-flop of their loafers coming up the stone path.

I have spent uncounted hours of my life in such haggard waiting, crazy in my conviction that they would never come back at all because something unspeakable had happened to them the way I had learned as a child that unspeakable things happen. And it has taken me years to understand that what I feared most of all was perhaps less the disaster that might have befallen them than the disaster of being locked up in the dark of my own fear. The Cowardly Lion. As one of the *Letters of the Scattered Brotherhood* puts it, "Your only safety is to be within the center of your kingdom, living from within out, not from without in."* I, on the other hand, lived so much from without in that I felt I had no safety at all unless I could be sure that my children were safe.

When they left home more or less for good, a whole new life had to begin without them. I soon discovered that for years most of what my wife and I had talked about had been the children—their comings and goings, what was happening in their lives. Now we had to discover new things to talk about. With just the two of us left among all those cluttered but empty rooms, we also had to make a new life together not unlike the way we did when we were first married. In addition to that, because neither of us could single-handedly fill for the other the empty place in ourselves left by the children's departure, we also had to

*Mary Strong, New York, Harper & Row, 1948, p. 53.

try to make new lives apart. My wife gave more time to the various environmental and conservationist organizations that she has believed in and worked for for a long time as well as to the running of the farm where we live—the flowers, the vegetable garden, the animals, the upkeep of the buildings. She has a quietness and patience inside herself that both nurtures and is nurtured by such quiet, patient things as those. She can lose herself and in some measure also find herself in them.

I on the other hand am an impatient person with little inner quietness. Vegetables take too long to grow and tend, animals too long to train and take care of. I need to have things as soon as I want them, need to have things going on, errands to run, places to go. I suppose because I spend so much of my life sitting alone in that barn-board paneled room with a notebook in my lap and a felt-tip pen in my hand what I need more than anything else is people—other lives to bounce my life off of and to share my life with, to give me life. So the way I tried to replace what the children had taken with them when they left, to find my way out of the Little Ease, which in many ways their leaving had precipitated me into, was to get out of the house more, to expand my horizons, to add to the cast of characters. I would go to the Grand Union to do the marketing the way I would go to a great museum—all those acres of jars, bottles, boxes, those glass-encased rarities of the deli counter, the glowing pigments of radish, eggplant, bean—or the way I would go to a great club—running into you never could tell just whom wheeling a cart toward you between dairy products and household wares, or shaking a honeydew to test for ripeness, or exchanging views with you on the human condition in the line at the checkout counter. But the time came when I needed more community even than that, and in the winter of 1982 I accepted an invitation to teach a course in preaching at Harvard Divinity School.

I attended Union Theological Seminary in New York City in the 1950s, and my years there were among the richest in my life. Reinhold Niebuhr was there then and so was Paul Tillich, Samuel Terrien, Paul Scherer, John Knox, George Buttrick, Robert Macafee Brown, and above all the great James Muilenburg, who more than any of them became my father and brother in Christ. But in addition to the excitement and challenge of those extraordinary teachers—I remember riding up in the elevator once with Paul Tillich so awed by his presence that I couldn't choke out so much as good morning—there was no less richly an extraordinary sense of community.

God knows there was nothing homogenous about the place. I can't think of a theological position or denominational affiliation that wasn't represented by one or the other of the men and women who had come to study there from almost every part of the country and every kind of background both intellectual and social. There were countless views on how the good news of the Gospel could be most authentically related to the headline news of those times when the Cold War was threatening to sweep civilization itself away under a final nuclear glacier and the civil rights movement was already beginning to burst into flame. But beneath all those ways in which we differed from one another there seemed to me to be something deep and life-giving that we all of us shared. Carved in wood over the door to the refectory were the words *Cognoverunt eum in fractionem panis* — they knew him in the breaking of the bread — and I had the feeling that in breaking bread together, in inching our way down the slow cafeteria line together, we found not only him as King and Christ but him as the elusive one whom, tatterdemalion crowd though we were, we all in our own ways loved and were hoping as best we could to serve. It was something like this that I went to Harvard hoping to find again, but though in other ways I found things of value there, in that way I have to admit that I found little or nothing.

I have no right to characterize the place as a whole because I never came to know the place as a whole. Once a week I drove the wintry road eastward over Bromley mountain and across the Connecticut River into New Hampshire and Massachusetts to teach the two sections of my course, and at the end of the day I drove home again. I rarely so much as laid eyes on any of my faculty colleagues let alone came to know them. I knew my students almost exclusively in the context of the classroom and nowhere else. I had no part in the routine of their lives. So I am willing to believe that all sorts of good things were going on among them elsewhere that I knew nothing about. In my own dealings with them, however, the things that I found going on were mostly just unexpected things.

In my days at Union, most teachers began their classes with a prayer, and I was always moved by the sight of them bowing their heads at the start of those little academic feasts in as homely and simple-hearted a way as they would have bowed them over turkey and creamed onions on Thanksgiving Day. So when I met my Harvard classes for the first time, I did the same thing. I forget what the prayer was—some prayerful hope, I suppose, that God would prosper the weeks we were to spend together—but apparently as soon as class was over the word went round like wildfire: He prayed! He prayed! I did not hear about the stir until later, but I must have sensed it at the time because almost from the first day I began to realize that it was not Union in 1954 but Harvard almost thirty years later.

Whatever may have bound my students together elsewhere in the way of common belief or commitment, I was much more aware of what divided them. It did not take me long to discover early in the game, as you might have thought I would have known before I came, that a number of them were Unitarian Universalists who by their own definition were humanist atheists. One of them, a woman about my age, came to see me in my office one day to say that although many of the things I had to teach about preaching she found interesting enough, few of them were of any practical use to people like her who did not believe in God. I asked her what it was she did believe in, and I remember the air of something like wistfulness with which she said that whatever it was, it was hard to put into words. I could sympathize with that, having much difficulty putting such things into words over the years myself, but at the same time I felt somehow floored and depressed by what she said. I think things like peace, kindness, social responsibility, honesty were the things she believed in—and maybe she was right, maybe that is the best there is to believe in and all there is—but it was hard for me to imagine giving sermons about such things. I could imagine lecturing about them or writing editorials about them, but I could not imagine standing up in a pulpit in a black gown with a stained glass window overhead and a Bible open on the lectern and the final chords of the sermon hymn fading away into the shadows and preaching about them. I realized that if ideas were all I had to preach, I would take up some other line of work.

I had never understood so clearly before what preaching is to me. Basically, it is to proclaim a Mystery before which, before whom, even our most exalted ideas turn to straw. It is also to proclaim this Mystery with a passion that ideas alone have little to do with. It is to try to put the Gospel into words not the way you would compose an essay but the way you would write a poem or a love letter—putting your heart into it, your own excitement, most of all your own life. It is to speak words that you hope may, by grace, be bearers not simply of new understanding but of new life both for the ones you are speaking to and also for you. Out of that life, who knows what new ideas about peace and honesty and social responsibility may come, but they are the fruits of the preaching, not the roots of it. Another Unitarian Universalist student said once that what he believed in was faith, and when I asked him faith in what, his answer was faith in faith. I don't mean to disparage him—he was doing the best he could—but it struck me that having faith in faith was as barren as being in love with love or having money that you spend only on the accumulation of more money. It struck me too that to attend a divinity school when you did not believe in divinity involved a peculiarly depressing form of bankruptcy, and there were times as I wandered through those corridors that I felt a little like Alice on the far side of the looking glass.

One of the readings I assigned was Shakespeare's *King Lear*, which I always assign in any course I teach about almost anything not only because I consider it by far Shakespeare's greatest play but also because it deals with the greatest of all questions, which is the question of the existence of God. After his enemies have plucked out his eyes, the Duke of Gloucester says, "As flies to wanton boys are we to the gods;/ They kill us for their sport," and after Cordelia has signed her own death warrant by returning from France to save her father, old Lear says, "Upon such sacrifices, my Cordelia,/ The Gods themselves throw incense." Either the power behind the scenes of the world is the cruel and idiot indifference of the wanton boys, or it is something like Cordelia's self-sacrificial love in giving her life to save the father who had disowned her. In exploring the depths of both of those possibilities, Shakespeare speaks with overwhelming honesty from which anyone who tries to preach the Gospel in a mad and fallen world has a crucial lesson to learn.

That was my reason for assigning the play to my students, but in addition to the Unitarian Universalists there was a committed group of feminists in the group one of whom said one day that she could not read the play because it was so full of sexist language, just as another objected later to reading G. K. Chesterton's *The Man Who Was Thursday* because all the main characters in it are men. Both of those women were right, of course—*Lear* is indeed full of sexist language and the seven members of the Central Anarchists Council are all male—but Chesterton wrote his novel in 1908 and Shakespeare his play about three hundred years earlier, and it seemed to me that if your principles keep you from being able to draw on the wisdom of writers of earlier generations who didn't happen to share those principles or even to be aware of them, you may keep your principles intact but at the same time do yourself a tragic disservice. It was a male student, deep into liberation theology, who found Graham Greene's *The Power and the Glory*, another novel I assigned, offensive because though it was set in the revolutionary Mexico of the 1930s it not only does not deal with the social and political issues for which that revolution was fought but makes the Judas figure a half-caste, which, as my student saw it, was an unpardonable example of racist thinking.

Harvard Divinity School was proud, and justly so, of what it called its pluralism—feminists, humanists, theists, liberation theologians all pursuing truth together—but the price that pluralism can cost was dramatized one day in a way that I have never forgotten. I had been speaking as candidly and personally as I knew how about my own faith and how I had tried over the years to express it in language. At the same time I had been trying to get the class to respond in kind. For the most part none of them were responding at all but just sitting there taking it in without saying a word. Finally I had to tell them what I thought. I said they reminded me of a lot of dead fish lying on cracked ice in a fish store window with their round blank eyes. There I was, making a fool of myself spilling out to them the secrets of my heart, and there they were, not telling me what they believed about anything beneath the level of their various causes. It was at that point that a black African student got up and spoke. "The reason I do not say anything about what I believe," he said in his stately African English, "is that I'm afraid it will be shot down."

At least for a moment we all saw, I think, that the danger of pluralism is that it becomes factionalism, and that if factions grind their separate axes too vociferously, something mutual, precious, and human is in danger of being drowned out and lost. I had good times as well as bad ones that winter term. I was able to say a few things that some of my students seemed to find valuable, and some of them said things that I value still, but if there was anything like a community to draw strength and comfort from there at Harvard as years before there had been at Union, I for one was not lucky enough to discover it.

We keep at our jobs whatever they happen to be. We keep the car in repair. We have the TV fixed and try to get the furnace cleaned once a year. We see to it that our clothes are reasonably clean and that there's something in the refrigerator for breakfast. We do the best we can taking care of the very young, the very old, and sometimes each other. If you have ever watched ants at work on a bare patch of lawn, you have seen us. They scurry this way, stop, scurry that way. They labor under the weight of the crumb they carry just so far before abandoning it. They meet and part, disappear into the grass and appear again or never do. Small things loom large—the fallen leaf, the rusty nail. Large things go unnoticed—the sky, the house, the enormous face in the air. They keep busy on their tiny errands. Life is busyness for all of us, is keeping busy. Keeping still comes harder. But stillness comes. Even the ant lays down her crumb. Even at our busiest and on the move, something within us pauses from time to time between the rusty nail and the fallen leaf, between stops on the subway, between laying down the pen and picking it up again. We keep still, and we dream. I don't know what dreams are, but I know they come from far away, both the sleeping kind and waking kind, and I know that at least some of them come from the gray chapel in the White Tower.

Somewhere around the time of that Harvard winter I dreamed I was staying in a hotel. I had a wonderful room where all was well with me and I was at peace. Then I left the hotel for some reason, and when I returned, I tried to get the same room back again except that I did not know where it was in the hotel. If it had a number, I didn't remember it. The man at the desk said he knew exactly the room I meant. He said all I had to do was ask for it by name. Then he told me the name. He said the name of the room where I had been at peace was Remember.

I think of all the things you and I could remember that would not bring us peace at all, but I believe that at least part of what the dream meant was that way beyond all those things, at the innermost heart, at the farthest reach, of our remembering, there is peace. The secret place of the Most High is there. Eden is there, the still waters, the green pastures. Home is there. I think our best dreams are always trying to move in that direction—homeward—and writing a novel, for me, is a form of dreaming, of deepest remembering. I dream up a character or two and some vague sense of a story to bring them together, and then, sitting on a couch with my feet propped on a low bench in front of me and my pen in my hand and my eyes staring out toward the window or down toward the slate floor, I let whatever wants to happen happen.

In the early eighties I made a number of false starts on novels. I would write about thirty pages or so and then lay them aside because they weren't coming to life for me. Most if not all of them, as I remember it now, had to do one way or another with Bermuda. That was where my dreams and remembering seemed to want to take me most. Bermuda was where we moved to in 1937 after my father's death, and in all those stillborn books I tried to describe what it had been like to live there more than half a century earlier when the most enchanted part of my childhood had followed hard on the heels of the saddest and darkest part.

It is hard to convey it to people who did not know it then because the Bermuda that existed before the Second World War does not exist anymore. There were no automobiles there or any other kind of motor vehicle. There was a small, narrow gauge railroad that ran from one end of the island to the other, and apart from that you either walked where you were going or rode your bicycle. If you could afford it, you might take a horse and carriage, either a Victoria with its hooded perambulator top that could be put up if it rained or a double carriage, which was a surrey with a fringed roof. There was also a small ferry that went from Hamilton to various points across the harbor including Paget where we lived in a pink house called The Moorings so near the water that my brother and I could fish off the terrace. The sounds of the island were the clip-clop of the horses and the silvery chime of bicycle bells and carriage bells. The smell of the island was mainly the smell of the dwarf cedars that grew everywhere then before they were destroyed by a blight, and the chalky smell of coral roads drying in the sun after a heavy, quick shower, and the smell of the ocean and the horses and the fields of Easter lilies that were grown commercially in those days. The color I remember best was the color of the Gulf Stream, which is the only thing that as far as I know remains unchanged—tawny in the shallows and then changing to celery green, emerald, turquoise blue, deep blue, as you moved out farther and deeper.

It was not just the beauty of the place that I tried to find words for but the feeling I can recapture to this day of living there and breathing that air. I remember the sound and feel of English money—the heavy coppers and florins and half crowns that weighed down your pockets, the thin little sixpences and threepenny bits, the pound notes with the King's picture on them. I remember the shops in Hamilton—like Trimingham's where you could buy Irish tweeds and cashmere sweaters and beautiful leather luggage, the bicycle shop full of slim Raleighs and Humbers and cedar handlebar baskets, and the Phoenix drugstore, fragrant, shadowy, with slow ceiling fans to stir the air. I remember the public library with a park behind it where a British regiment called the Sherwood Foresters gave band concerts underneath a huge India rubber tree, and a bookstore that smelled the way a new book printed in England does when you first open it. I remember Warwick Academy where my brother and I went to school—flying kites on Good Friday, lighting bonfires on all the hills in Bermuda to celebrate the coronation of George the Sixth.

I had happy times as a child before Bermuda, but the times I remember best from those earlier years are mostly somber ones—my father moving from job to job and my father's drinking, which changed him from a gentle, conscientious man to a flamboyant, fragmented one; and my mother with her discontent and her terrible tongue; and worst of all the appalling sound of their voices raised in anger as they fought about God only knows what or to what dread end. Because we moved to a different town, a different house, a different school almost every year, those two people were the only fixed home I had, and I knew that if something awful happened between them or to them, the awful thing that would happen to me was that I would have no other place not only to go but even to *be*. When my father wrote in his suicide note to my mother, "I love and adore you but am no good," I can only assume he believed that we would be better off without him, and in a tragic way he was right. In that way his death was, as I suspect he intended it to be, his last, best gift to us. It was also about the only gift he had left by then to give.

In any case, all that somberness ended with the end of my father, and the brightness and peace of the island we moved to were only the outward and visible signs of a brightness and peace that opened up inside my ten-year-old self. Naya came with us. Naya was the grandmother name we gave to my mother's mother who was half French-Swiss and half old New England. She loved books and music and the French language and managed somehow to be so at peace inside herself that even when the heavens were falling, she could sit smoking a Chesterfield in a white paper holder and never turn a hair. She was my one true parent in the sense that she loved me not for the extent to which I filled her need but simply for the pleasure of having somebody sixty years younger than she was to love. She played wistful tunes on the piano with one finger. She told marvelous stories about the past. She wore her hair in a bun and every once in a great while would make a French veal stew that left the kitchen looking like the scene of a massacre. So it was Naya and my mother, my brother and I who aboard the Monarch of Bermuda landed in Hamilton Harbor for the first time in the midst of a tropical shower the winter of 1937 and with all our luggage took a carriage to where we were going to start our new lives. The driver put up the hooded Victoria top and snapped a black rubber sheet across us to keep out the wet. I remember the horse-drawn traffic clattering all around us, the anvil ring of the great hoofs on the cobblestones, the fragrance of the rain on paw paws, horse manure, hedges of oleander and hibiscus, the glistening of the rain on the steaming flanks of the horse and the driver's rubber cape. More than anything else I remember to the point of being able to feel echoes of it to this day the almost unbearable lurch of freedom and gladness and wild excitement in my stomach as we trotted off around the harbor.

Fifty years later Bermuda was where most of those unfinished novels were set, and as I think back on them now, it seems clear that in the process of trying to remember and dream my way into them, what I was looking for was less a book about that enchanted place to write than a place like that enchanted place inside myself to find and be.

THREE *The Basement Room*

"ALMIGHTY God, unto whom all hearts are open, all desires known, and from whom no secrets are hid; cleanse the thoughts of our hearts by the inspiration of thy Holy Spirit, that we may perfectly love thee, and worthily magnify thy holy Name; through Christ our Lord. Amen."

Our secrets are not hid from God, says the ancient collect, but they are hid from each other, and some of them we so successfully hide even from ourselves that after a while we all but forget they exist. If somebody had asked me as a little boy of eight or nine, say, what my secrets were, I wonder if I would have thought to list among them a father who at parties drank himself into a self I could hardly recognize as my father, and a mother who in her rage could say such wild and scathing things to him that it made the very earth shake beneath my feet when I heard them, and a two-and-a-half years younger brother who for weeks at a time would refuse to get out of bed because bed, I suspect, was the only place he knew in the whole world where he felt safe. I knew that my father's suicide was a secret when that time came, but it was only a great deal later still that I realized that his life too had become a secret, almost the very fact that he had existed at all—the way he had looked and talked, the way it had felt to be with him, the way it had felt to be without him, back there at the start, before I had learned that the rule was that I was not to speak about such feelings and thus finally lost them to silence. I hear the self-pity in that, but I do not apologize for it. I pity that child who happens to have been me the way I would pity any child under similar circumstances. That child was among other things pitiable, and to see him otherwise would be not to see him whole. We are commanded to love our neighbors as ourselves, and I believe that to love ourselves means to extend to those various selves that we have been along the way the same degree of compassion and concern that we would extend to anyone else. If to do so is unseemly, then so much the worse for seemliness.

For people born more or less when I was and into more or less the same sociological corner of things, sex too became a secret, of course, when that time came around—the fierce hunger of the flesh both to give and to receive pleasure, the terror of sex, the confusion of it, the animal innocence and joy of it more often than not lost in what was apt to seem the shame and shabbiness of it, or foregone altogether out of timidity or fear. I suppose sex is the secret that to one degree or another we all of us keep from each other, more then than now needless to say—the great open secret that, whatever else we are, we are bodies and that as bodies we need to touch and be touched by each other as much as we need to laugh and cry and play and talk and work with each other. Once they had sinned, Adam and Eve tried to hide their nakedness from each other and from God, and to one degree or another we have all been hiding it ever since for the reason, I suppose, that we know that our sexuality is yet another good gift from God which as sinners we can nonetheless use to dehumanize both each other and ourselves.

And then when I married and had children, there were all the secrets of that new family which my wife and I had created, secrets rooted deep, of course, in the secrets of the two families that had created the two of us. What, for one, was the secret that was too dark or dangerous or private or complicated to tell in any other language which our daughter could bring herself to talk about only in the symbolic language of anorexia? Why did my mother close her eyes when she talked to us—what secret was she trying to close in, what invasion of her secrecy was she trying to close out? I, with my eyes wide open, closed my eyes for years to the secret that I was looking to my children to give me more than either they had it in their power to give or could have given without somehow crippling themselves in the process. I thought that what I was afraid of more than anything else was that something awful would happen to them, but the secret I began to glimpse was that I was really less afraid for the children than I was afraid for myself. What awful thing would happen to me if something happened to them—that was what I was afraid of. What dangerous and unknown new role might I fall into if the role of father were taken from me and suddenly the sky was the limit, if instead of trying to take care of my children's needs, I started taking care of my own needs, some of which were so powerful and long neglected that I was afraid they might overwhelm me? It was the Little Ease of my own fear that I was afraid of most, I think, because there was no room to live and move there or to have any being worthy of the name.

"Cleanse the thoughts of our hearts by the inspiration of thy Holy Spirit," the collect goes, "that we may perfectly love" if not thee, because we are such a feckless and faithless crowd most of us, then at least ourselves, at least each other. If, as someone has said, we are as sick as our secrets, then to get well is to air those secrets if only in our own hearts, which the prayer asks God himself to air and cleanse. When our secrets are guilty secrets, like the burden I had unwittingly placed on my own children, we can start to make amends, to change what can be changed; we can start to heal. When they are sad and hurtful secrets, like my father's death, we can in a way honor the hurt by letting ourselves feel it as we never let ourselves feel it before, and then, having felt it, by laying it aside; we can start to take care of ourselves the way we take care of people we love. To love our neighbors as we love ourselves means also to love ourselves as we love our neighbors. It means to treat ourselves with as much kindness and understanding as we would the person next door who is in trouble. Little by little then we begin to be able to look at each other's faces, and at our own faces in the mirror, without the intervening shadows that unaired secrets cast. We begin to find a source of new life in what the 91st Psalm calls "the secret place of the Most High," which I believe dwells in all of us as the image of God and in which I believe some part of all of us dwells. It is precisely that secret and holy place which I believe I glimpsed in the Norman chapel of Saint John, and caught some bright foreshadowing of as a child in Bermuda, and dreamed of once as a room called Remember. The reason I was so at peace in that room, I think, is that in it I remembered back before time and beyond space to the day when God in his glory made us and the morning stars sang together and all the sons of God shouted for joy. By quieting our minds and keeping still, by praying less in words perhaps than in images, maybe most of all by just letting up on ourselves and letting go, I think we can begin to put ourselves back in touch with that glory and joy we come from and begin moving out of the shadows toward something more like light.

As for me, in the fall of 1985 I moved west. All my life I have been an easterner. I think of the East as more than anything else coastal. I think of it as where the cold winds of the sea strike first, where the winds of change, of new ideas, of foreignness, strike first, and where if war ever comes, I suppose the bombs will strike first too. I think of the East as the outer edge of things where there is always the danger of losing your foothold on the reality and reliability and Americanness of things and falling off the edge. As I drove due west from Albany, I had an almost physical sensation of traveling in what was for me the right direction although it was only later that I thought I saw why. I came to believe that there are reasons other than geographical for calling the Middle West the heartland of this country. It seemed to me closer to the heart of the American past—Chicago reminded me of the New York of my childhood, with men going to work in hats and ties, women wearing stockings and carrying purses—closer to the heart of whatever it is that is most American about America, to the workaday human values that held this country together when the wilderness was still out there somewhere west of the Mississippi instead of right here inside ourselves.

The place I was heading for was Wheaton College in Wheaton, Illinois, about an hour west of Chicago. They have a great collection there of the manuscripts and papers of people like C. S. Lewis, G. K. Chesterton, George MacDonald, J. R. R. Tolkien, Dorothy Sayers, and the like, and because I could think of no more distinguished company than theirs among whom to have my own literary remains molder, a year earlier I had offered them everything I had stowed away over the years in cardboard boxes and scrapbooks and manilla folders; and to my delight they said that they would be delighted to have it. They even went so far as to have a small ceremony of dedication at the library, which I attended and during the course of which Lyle Dorsett gave me my first tour of the Wade collection including the wardrobe, built by Lewis's grandfather

Hamilton, through which the Pevensie children make their initial sally into the land of Narnia. Someone told me that while Lewis was still living at the Kilns, he was awakened one night by a terrible racket only to discover that a visiting child had climbed into the wardrobe and was trying to beat his own way into Narnia through the back of it just as, if I'd thought I had half a chance, I would have been tempted to do then and there myself. In any case, it was on the occasion of that visit that Beatrice Batson, the chairman of the English department, who like Lyle Dorsett and his wife Mary has since become my good friend, invited me to give a course at Wheaton for a semester, and when the time came, I drove off to teach it almost as totally ignorant of what I would find when I got there as when I had gone to Harvard a few years earlier.

I knew it was Billy Graham's alma mater. I knew it was evangelical though without any clear idea as to what that meant. I knew that, although as only a visiting professor I would myself be exempt from it, everyone had to sign a pledge not to smoke or drink for as long as they either taught or studied there. If I had known that they had to pledge also not to dance, of all things, I think that I would probably have been horrified enough to turn down the invitation on principle. The irony is that if I had done so, my life would have been immeasurably impoverished.

The famous pledge sends out highly misleading signals not only as to what Christianity is all about but also as to what Wheaton College is all about. Because of those signals I was apprehensive about having my students read *The Brothers Karamazov* as I had planned. I was afraid that Ivan's devastating attack on belief in a loving God might constitute a heresy that the administration would not tolerate, and then I discovered that it was one of the standard texts used in the English Department. Whatever evangelical meant, in other words, it did not mean closed minded. On the contrary I found the college as open to what was going on in the world and as generally sophisticated as any I have known. What made it different from any I have known can perhaps best be suggested by the college motto, which is more in evidence there than such mottos usually are. It is not in Latin like most of the other mottos I can think of but in English plain enough for anybody to read and understand. "For Christ and his Kingdom" is the way it goes—as plain as that.

I do not want to idealize the place. The pledge was not the only thing about it that I found a little suffocating, clubbishly holier-than-thou, legalistic. For instance I remember a class discussion of Alice Walker's *The Color Purple* one day. There was one aspect of it that most of the students simply couldn't deal with, and that was that humanly speaking Celie's soul was undeniably saved by her friendship with her friend Shug and at the same time that the friendship had a sexual side to it. Homosexuality, in their book, was unqualifiably Bad, but the reclamation of Celie was unqualifiably Good, and they simply could not put the two together. I argued that when Jesus says, "You shall love the Lord your God with all your

80

heart . . . and your neighbor as yourself . . . on these two commandments depend all the law and the prophets," he meant that by this one great law of love all lesser laws are judged including the ones against homosexuality, which the students pointed out to me in the pages of Scripture but which in the case of Celie, I tried to point out to them, the law of love clearly superseded. The class was divided on the issue and feelings ran high, but for a wonder nobody got mad at anybody. It is less of a wonder that few of the opposition were convinced by my argument, but as far as I could tell, none of them got mad at me either.

All this to the contrary notwithstanding, it seemed to me that insofar as their resounding motto can be true of any institution, it was true of Wheaton. Literature, history, science, the arts—as nearly as I could tell, everything that was taught there was taught from the perspective of Christian faith and for the purpose of enriching and deepening that faith. It would be easy to belittle such an approach to education as narrowly limiting and parochial, but I found it moving and refreshing especially when compared to the approach of the great eastern universities that I have had dealings with whose mottos echo a faith that has long since become as obsolete in their scheme of things as the Latin they are written in.

One day I was having lunch with two students who were talking about whatever they were talking about—the weather, the movies—when without warning one of them asked the other as naturally as he would have asked the time of day what God was doing in his life. If there is anything in this world I believe, it is that God is indeed doing all kinds of things in the lives of all of us including those who do not believe in God and would have nothing to do with him if they did, but in the part of the East where I live, if anybody were to ask a question like that, even among religious people, the sky would fall, the walls would cave in, the grass would wither. I think the very air would stop my mouth if I opened it to speak such words among just about any group of people I can think of in the East because their faith itself, if they happen to have any, is one of the secrets that they have kept so long that it might almost as well not exist. The result was that to find myself at Wheaton among people who, although they spoke about it in different words from mine and expressed it in their lives differently, not only believed in Christ and his Kingdom more or less as I did but were also not ashamed or embarrassed to say so was like finding something which, only when I tasted it, I realized I had been starving for for years.

I also found myself going to an extraordinary church or, with my rather dim experience of churches back home, one that was extraordinary at least to me. Its name was Saint Barnabas, and it was located in a small town nearby called Glen Ellyn. It was described to me as an evangelical high Episcopal church, and that seemed so wonderfully anomalous that what took me there first was pure curiosity. What kept taking me back Sunday after Sunday, however, was something else again. Part of the service was chanted at

Saint Barnabas, and I discovered that when a prayer or a psalm or a passage from the Gospels is sung, you hear it in a new way. Words wear thin after a while, especially religious words. We have spoken them and listened to them so often that after a while we hardly even hear them any more. As writer, preacher, teacher I have spent so much of my life dealing with words that I find I get fed up with them. I get fed up especially with my own words and the sound of my own voice endlessly speaking them. What the chanting did was to remind me that worship is more than words and then in a way to give words back to me again. It reminded me that words are not only meaning but music and magic and power. The chanting italicized them, made poetry of their prose. It helped me hear the holiness in them and in all of us as we chanted them.

They also used incense at Saint Barnabas. They censed the open pages of the Gospel before they read from it, and even in the midst of a midwestern October heat wave, the church was suddenly filled with Christmas. The hushed fragrance of it, the thin haze of it, seemed to say that it is not just to our minds that God seeks to make himself known, because, whatever we may think, we are much more than just our minds, but to our sense of touch and taste too, to our seeing and hearing and smelling the air whether it is incense that the air is laden with or burning leaves or baking bread or honest human sweat. "O taste and see that the Lord is good!" says the 34th Psalm, and it is not just being metaphorical.

Most evangelical preaching that I have heard is seamless, hard sell, and heavily exhortatory. Men in business suits get up and proclaim the faith with the dynamic persuasiveness of insurance salesmen. If there are any evangelical women preachers, I have never happened to come across them. The churches these preachers get up in are apt to be large, packed full, and so brilliantly lit that you feel there is no mystery there that has not been solved, no secrets there that can escape detection. Their sermons couldn't be more different from the generally low-key ones that I am used to in the sparsely attended churches of New England, but they give me the same sense of being official, public, godly utterances which the preacher stands *behind* but as a human being somehow does not stand *in*. Whatever passionate and private experience their sermons may have come from originally, you are given little or no sense of what that private experience was. At their best they bring many strengths with them into the pulpit but rarely, as I listened to them anyway, their real lives.

In that sense at least the rector of Saint Barnabas, a man named Robert MacFarlane, did not strike me as evangelical at all. His sermons were not seamless and armor plated but had spaces in them, spaces of silence as if he needed those spaces to find deep within himself what he was going to say next, as if he was giving the rest of us space to think for a moment about what he had just been trying to say last. There was never any doubt in my mind but that the faith he was laying out before us was a faith that, even as he spoke it, he was drawing out of the raw stuff of his own life. He spoke very quietly, and the church he spoke in was not brilliantly lit but full of shadow, full of secrets.

One particular sermon I will always remember though I cannot be sure that it is exactly the sermon he preached because of course it is the sermons we preach to ourselves around the preacher's sermons that are the ones that we hear most powerfully. He was talking about Saint Peter in any case, how Peter was sitting outside in the high priest's courtyard while Jesus was inside being interrogated. A maidservant came up and asked him if it wasn't true that he was a follower of this man who was at the root of all the trouble. Then Peter said, "I do not know the man." It was Peter's denial, of course, MacFarlane said: *I do not even know who he is*. It was the denial that Jesus himself had predicted, and the cock raised his beak into the air and crowed just as Jesus had foretold. But it was something else too, MacFarlane said. It was a denial, but it was also the truth. Peter really did not know who Jesus was, did not really know, and neither do any of us really know who Jesus is either. Beyond all we can find to say about him and believe about him, he remains always beyond our grasp, except maybe once in a while the hem of his garment. We should never forget that. We can love him, we can learn from him, but we can come to know him only by following him—by searching for him in his church, in his Gospels, in each other. That was the sermon I heard anyway, and I remember thinking that if it were not for all the reasons I have for living where I do, I could imagine moving a thousand miles just to be near where I could hear truth spoken like that. And I remember too that the last time I attended a service there, there were real tears running down my cheeks at the realization that the chances were I would probably never find myself there again. When I got home, I thought I could not rest until I found a church like that.

I never did find one, any more than I have ever found again a community of faith like Wheaton, and because life always gets in the way of living, and there are always so many things to do, so many places to go, I never really looked that hard either, or looked in the wrong places. One of the places I looked was a Greek Orthodox monastery not far from our Vermont house where my wife and I attended mass one Sunday morning. The vestments were far more gorgeous than those of Saint Barnabas and both the chanting and the incense just as rich, but there the comparison ended. It was the monks who conducted the moving and glittering ceremony whereas the congregation just sat or stood on the sidelines watching the splendor of it but without, as far as my experience went anyway, having any very satisfactory part in it. I felt like a child with his nose pressed to a bakery shop window—impressed by what I saw but a little lonely and unnourished. The sermon, on the other hand, was one that I will long remember. It was preached by a huge monk in cloth of gold, and his point was that there are many people in this world who do not realize how impoverished they are spiritually. "Even a dog knows when it is uncomfortable" was a phrase he used, but we whose spiritual discomfort is apt to be so profound are in many cases entirely unaware of it.

I did not find another Saint Barnabas but I did find another saint whom I made the hero of another novel, which maybe in a way was about just such searching and not finding as I had been involved in at the monastery although the thought never occurred to me then. This time it was a sixth-century Irish saint known as Brendan the Navigator, who spent much of his life sailing the seas in a curragh made of wicker and leather in search of the Terrestrial Paradise of Tir-na- n-Og or the Land of the Blessed, which he believed lay out there somewhere beyond the western horizon. He was a haggard sort of man as I pictured him, in many of the ways that I also am haggard, a loose-footed sort of a red-headed, inhibited, nimble-tongued, miracle-working man. He may have sailed as far as Newfoundland in his wanderings, maybe even as far as Florida some believe, but he never found what he was after, needless to say, and at the end of his long life somewhere around the year 580 wondered if perhaps he had spent all those years on a wild goose chase when he might better have stayed home and looked for Christlier ways to serve Christ and his Kingdom there. He meets the Welsh historian-monk Gildas one day, and when Gildas stands up at the end of their interview to dismiss him, the narrator of the novel, a friend of Brendan's named Finn, describes what happened like this:

For the first time we saw he wanted one leg. It was gone from the knee joint down. He was hopping sideways to reach for his stick in the corner when he lost his balance. He would have fallen in a heap if Brendan hadn't leapt forward and caught him.

"I'm as crippled as the dark world," Gildas said.

"If it comes to that, which one of us isn't, my dear?" Brendan said.

Gildas with but one leg. Brendan sure he'd misspent his whole life entirely. Me that had left my wife to follow him and buried our only boy. The truth of what Brendan said stopped all our mouths. We was cripples all of us. For a moment or two there was no sound but the bees.

"To lend each other a hand when we're falling," Brendan said. "Perhaps that's the only work that matters in the end."

"The Kingdom of God is among you," Jesus said—the Land of the Blessed—and possibly he was saying something at least like the same thing. It is not beyond the western horizon that the Kingdom lies but among you, among ourselves, within ourselves and our lives together.

Brendan was published by Atheneum in 1987, and since then HarperCollins has brought it out in paperback. For some time now Clayton Carlson, who is in charge of their religion division, in addition to publishing all of my nonfiction, has brought out paperback editions of virtually all of my earlier books which I would want to keep in print. His view is that a publisher publishes writers rather than just books, and thanks to him words I wrote as long as twenty-five years ago or so, which otherwise would have long since fallen into oblivion, continue to find new readers.

I did not find another Saint Barnabas, but I found Saint Brendan, and then by luck or by grace I found something else too although not in the place I would have expected to find it. Consider again those dwarves in C. S. Lewis's *The Last Battle*. They are huddled together in what they think is a cramped, dark, stable where, like the dungeon of the Little Ease, there is hardly any room to move or breathe. The truth of it, you will remember, is that they are not in any such place at all. Instead they are in the midst of an endless green meadow where the sun is shining and the sky is blue. Aslan himself stands there offering them refreshments and freedom from their self-imprisonment, the great golden Lion who moves through Lewis's fairytale the way the fierce power of God moves through our world of Cowardly Lions—to be called "Dear heart" by whom is an everlasting blessing and to be rebuked by whom is an everlasting shame. But the dwarves see none of this. About all they can see is each other.

Now transform that scene. It is not Lewis's dwarves who are gathered together. It is people very much like you and me. They are sitting in the basement of a church or an American Legion post or an after-hours hospital cafeteria. Fluorescent lights buzz overhead. There is an urn of coffee. There is a basket which is passed around at some point which everybody who can afford to puts a dollar in to help pay for the coffee and the rent of the room. In one sense they are strangers who know each other only by their first names and almost nothing else about each other. In another sense they are best friends who little by little come to know each other from the inside out instead of the other way round, which is the way we usually do it. They do not know each other's biographies, but they know something about each other's frailties, failures, fears. They know something too about each other's strengths, hopes, gladness and about where they have found them. They do not give each other advice. They simply give each other stories about the good and the bad of what has happened to them over the years. Though they do not use such images to describe it, they tell each other of the glimpses they have had from time to time of the sunlit meadow beyond the confining dark, of the great Lion who from time to time has stooped his golden head and breathed on them. In other words, they tell each other their secrets, and as you listen to them, you hear among other things your own secrets on their lips.

They could hardly be a more ill-assorted lot. Some are educated, and some never finished grade school. Some are on welfare, and some of them have hit the jackpot. Some are straight, and some are gay. There are senior citizens among them and also twenty-year-olds. Some groups are composed of alcoholics and some, like the ones I found my way to, of people who have no alcoholic problem themselves but come from families who did. The one thing they have in common can be easily stated. It is just that

they all believe that they cannot live fully human
lives without each other and without what they call
their Higher Power. They avoid using the word *God*
because some of them do not believe in God. What
they all do believe in, or are searching for, is a power
higher than their own which will make them well.
Some of them would simply say that it is the power of
the group itself.

They are apt to begin their meetings with a prayer
written by my old seminary professor Reinhold
Niebuhr: "God, grant me the serenity to accept the
things I cannot change, the courage to change the
things I can, and wisdom to know the difference."
They are apt to end with the Lord's Prayer: "*thy* will be
done . . . give us *this* day our daily bread . . . forgive
us as we forgive . . . deliver us." "To lend each other a
hand when we're falling," Brendan said. "Perhaps
that's the only work that matters in the end." As they
live their lives, they try to follow a kind of spiritual
rule, which consists basically not only of uncovering
their own deep secrets but of making peace with the
people they have hurt and been hurt by. Through
prayer and meditation, through seeking help from
each other and from helpful books, they try to draw
near any way they can to God or to whatever they call
what they have instead of God. They sometimes make
serious slips. They sometimes make miraculous
gains. They laugh a lot. Once in a while they cry.
When the meeting is over, some of them embrace.
Sometimes one of them will take special responsibil-

ity for another, agreeing to be available at any hour of day or night if the need should arise.

They also have slogans, which you can either dismiss as hopelessly simplistic or cling on to like driftwood in a stormy sea. One of them is "Let go and let God"—which is so easy to say and for people like me so far from easy to follow. Let go of the dark, which you wrap yourself in like a straitjacket, and let in the light. Stop trying to protect, to rescue, to judge, to manage the lives around you—your children's lives, the lives of your husband, your wife, your friends—because that is just what you are powerless to do. Remember that the lives of other people are not your business. They are their business. They are God's business because they all have God whether they use the word God or not. Even your own life is not your business. It also is God's business. Leave it to God. It is an astonishing thought. It can become a life-transforming thought.

Go where your best prayers take you. Unclench the fists of your spirit and take it easy. Breathe deep of the glad air and live one day at a time. Know that you are precious. Remember the license plate and learn to trust. Know that you can trust God. Know that you can trust these people with your secrets because they have trusted you with theirs. The meeting in the basement begins with all of you introducing yourselves. "I am Fred . . . I am Mary . . . I am Scotty," you say, and each time the rest of the group responds with "Hi, Fred . . . Hi, Mary . . . Hi, Scotty." Just by getting yourself there and saying that, you have told an extremely important secret, which is that you cannot go it alone. You need help. You need them. You need whatever name you choose to give the One whom Lewis named Aslan. "Have no anxiety about anything, but in everything by prayer and supplication make your requests known to God. And the peace that passes all understanding will keep your hearts and minds in Christ Jesus." (Philippians 3:6–7)

I do not believe that such groups as these which I found my way to not long after returning from Wheaton, or Alcoholics Anonymous, which is the group they all grew out of, are perfect any more than anything human is perfect, but I believe that the church has an enormous amount to learn from them. I also believe that what goes on in them is far closer to what Christ meant his church to be, and what it originally was, than much of what goes on in most churches I know. These groups have no buildings or official leadership or money. They have no rummage sales, no altar guilds, no every-member canvases. They have no preachers, no choirs, no liturgy, no real estate. They have no creeds. They have no program. They make you wonder if the best thing that could happen to many a church might not be to have its building burn down and to lose all its money. Then all that the people would have left would be God and each other.

The church often bears an uncomfortable resemblance to the dysfunctional family. There is the authoritarian presence of the minister—the professional who knows all of the answers and calls most of the shots—whom few ever challenge either because they don't dare to or because they feel it would do no good if they did. There is the outward camaraderie and inward loneliness of the congregation. There are the unspoken rules and hidden agendas, the doubts and disagreements that for propriety's sake are kept more or less under cover. There are people with all sorts of enthusiasms and creativities which are not often enough made use of or even recognized because the tendency is not to rock the boat but to keep on doing things the way they have always been done.

These groups I speak of, on the other hand, are more like what families at their best can be than most families are, certainly more than what the family I grew up in myself ever was. They are more like families because in them something which is often extraordinarily like truth is spoken in something that is extraordinarily like love. They are more like families because if ever the members of AA or Alanon or Adult Children of Alcoholics or the rest of them find themselves in trouble almost anywhere in the world, they know that they will find people there who are less like strangers than like sisters and brothers and who will offer them a degree of human understanding and practical help which I am afraid most church-goers would rarely be apt to go to a church to find and which I'm afraid most churches would rarely know how to give them in the event that they did. "Adult children" is an odd phrase meaning adults who still carry within them many of the confusions and fears and hurts of their childhood, and one of the luckiest things I ever did, to use one kind of language — one of

God's most precious gifts to me, to use another—was to discover that I was one of them and that there were countless others like me who were there when I needed them and by whom I also was needed. I have found more spiritual nourishment and strength and understanding among them than I have found anywhere else for a long time.

I make it sound as though my life was very purposeful during this time—as though everything I did was geared toward some conscious goal. That is a long way from being the truth of it as far as I can recapture the truth of it. Beneath the surface of my life I think maybe a kind of purposefulness was working itself out in spite of me. So much of who all of us are seems to go on down there—the dreams we have, the impulses, the hunches, the changes of mood. Often the decisions we think we make on the spur of the moment have been years in the making, and plans that we suddenly change were plans that we secretly abandoned long before. But *on* the surface instead of beneath it—in terms of my life as I was more or less aware of living it—I was no more purposeful than a dog sniffing its way down the street. I lived not from the inside out, as one of the brotherhood's scattered letters put it, but from the outside in. I responded to whatever came up. I followed the scents of happenstance.

Two people I loved died—one of them was my friend Dudley Knott, whose heart simply stopped beating one night while he was asleep—and the other was my mother-in-law, Serena Merck, who was not only a great lady, which is one thing, but also a good woman, which is another. I asked her once when she was laid low by congestive heart failure and could hardly speak above a whisper if there was anything she would like me to read out loud to her, thinking that as a Christian Scientist she might say something out of Mary Baker Eddy or the Bible maybe. What she did say was that, yes, she would. She asked me to find a copy of that morning's *New York Times* financial section and read to her how Archer Daniels was doing. Up to only a day or two of her death, she held fast to the world not because she was afraid to leave it or wasn't prepared to leave it but because she enjoyed it so much she just did not want to leave it. One or the other of her octogenarian friends would come perch on the side of her bed, and they would play cards together there when she could hardly hold the cards — the old friend peering through her cataract lenses to try to tell hearts from diamonds and my mother-in-law, in her diamonds, breathing through the tube that connected her with the oxygen cylinder which kept up the beating of her heart. The last time I can remember perching on the side of her bed myself, I asked her an utterly absurd question which happened to occur to me. If she could be any letter of the alphabet she wanted to be, I said, which letter would she choose. The answer she gave me was so faint that I had to bend down to hear. It was the letter Z. She wanted to be the *last* letter, in other words. She wanted to stick around as long as she could possibly stick it — partly, my guess is, because she thought it would be a plug for Christian Science but mostly, I'm sure, because even when her time had all but run out, she was still having a good time. She was still managing even to give a good time.

She died at the age of eighty-seven in her house in southern Florida, and for the last few years my wife and I have taken to spending winters down there ourselves though for a long time we looked down our noses at such people as weaklings and traitors. Our house looks out on the Atlantic Ocean, and after so many years of living in the Vermont mountains, which let you see only as far as they want you to see, there is something that wonderfully feeds the spirit in the sheer horizontalness of it. It lets you see as far as the eye can travel — as if there is nothing you have to do, nothing you have to be, more than simply travel with your eyes out over the endless waters farther than even Brendan ever sailed. Florida is in a hundred ways a crazy place to live — geriatric, impossibly commercialized and overdeveloped, neither the North nor the South — but it is full of people my age and considerably older who are there mainly just to enjoy themselves. There is of course something in all of us that recoils at that as indefensible and unchristian in a world full of suffering, but I think there is something else you can say about it too. The world is full of suffering indeed, and to turn our backs on it is to work a terrible unkindness maybe almost more on ourselves than on the world. But life indeed is also to be enjoyed. I suspect that may even be the whole point of it. I more than suspect that is why all the sons of God shouted for joy when he first brought it into being. And if that is the case, then the old woman playing shuffleboard in the sun and the young man standing in line with his children to get into Disney World are in their own ways praising God as truly as when they are serving supper in a shelter for the homeless or driving off at two thirty in the morning to answer the panicky phone call of an alcoholic friend.

It was in Florida too that I started going to see another therapist who was herself an adult child and whom I suppose for that reason I was able to listen to and learn from in ways that I had not found possible when I had tried therapy some years earlier. A lot of what she did was not just to help me remember forgotten parts of my childhood and to recapture some of the feelings connected with them, which I had discovered as a child that I would do well to forget, but also to suggest certain techniques for accomplishing that. One such technique that worked especially well for me was writing about those distant days with my left hand. My right hand is my grown-up hand—a writer's hand, a minister's hand—but when I wrote with the left hand, I found that what tended to come out was as artless and basic as the awkward scrawl it came out in. It was as if some of my secrets had at last found a way of communicating with me directly. She suggested on one occasion that when I got home I should try writing out a dialogue with my father, using my left hand for both of our parts, and here is part of how it went:

The Basement Room

CHILD: How are you?

FATHER: I am fine.

CHILD: Long time no see.

FATHER: It's been a long time.

CHILD: Do you remember the last time we saw each other? Jamie and I in Essex Fells that morning in November?

FATHER: I remember. You were playing a game. Everybody was asleep.

CHILD: Were you very sad? Were you scared, Daddy? Did you know what you were going to do?

FATHER: I had to do it. Things were so bad there wasn't any good way out.

CHILD: Could I have stopped you, Daddy? If I'd told you I loved you? If I told you how I needed you?

* * * * * * *

FATHER: No nobody could. I was lost so badly.

* * * * * * *

CHILD: Is this really you I'm talking to? I can't see your face. I've forgotten your voice, your smell.

FATHER: I remember you. I was proud of you. I wanted you to like me.

* * * * * * *

CHILD: I've been so worried. I've been so scared ever since.

FATHER: Don't be. There is nothing to worry about. That is the secret I never knew, but I know it now.

CHILD: What do you know, Daddy? . . . my dearest
Dad and father?

FATHER: I know plenty, and it's all good. I will see you
again. Be happy, for me. It is my birthday
present to you . . . I loved you boys. I love you
still.

CHILD: I love you . . . Goodbye for now.

FATHER: So long, Fritz. Everything is going to be all
right.

I don't know what that proves if it proves a
blessed thing. Probably the most it proves is that the
little left-handed game worked by helping me dredge
things up out of myself that maybe I wouldn't have
had access to any other way. But I couldn't help wondering at the time, as I can't help wondering still now,
if just maybe—"There are more things in heaven and
earth, Horatio,/Than are dreamt of in your philoso-
phy."—in some sense it really was my father I was talking to. Who knows? Who can say for sure either way?
But even if it was not really my father, what it was
most really was a better way of saying so long to him
than I had ever been able to say it before.

It was in another way that I said so long also to
my mother. A few months after she died, I had a
dream about her. The dream was set in the bedroom
of her apartment on 79th Street, only the room had
been cleared at last of all the years of her accumulat-
ing. The furniture, the pictures, the things under
beds and in closets, the clothes, the boxes, the old
letters—they were all gone. It was superbly empty

now. The walls and ceiling had been repainted white.
The floors had been waxed and polished. The dusty
Venetian blinds were gone, and the sunlight came
slanting in through the windows and made clear, ge-
ometric shapes on the bare walls. All the dramas that
had taken place were over and done with. All the life
my mother had lived there and the death she had
died there were over and done with too. I thought
how now there could be new tenants there, new life.
Then suddenly my mother was there, and my brother,
Jamie, and I were there with her. My brother reached
out and patted her as she went by as if to show me she
was real. She was paying no particular attention to either of us. She looked very well, in her thirties or
early forties maybe. She was getting ready to go out
someplace, and all her energies were being devoted to
that end. She was fussing about her hair, her clothes.
She said she had to meet a woman somewhere and
didn't want to be late. She even named the woman,
who was somebody I knew she had particularly dis-
liked for over sixty years, which helps me believe that
maybe the Kingdom of Heaven was where she was
and is. That is all I can remember her saying, and that
is about all there was to the dream.

It didn't seem a very important dream to me at the
time, but what it said to me was important. I think it
said that my mother was somehow back in business.
It said that there was no need to worry about her anymore. When she was alive, the rule she laid down—
all the more devastatingly by of course never saying it
in so many words—was that my brother and I had no

right to be happy as long as she was unhappy. The dream said that that was over with now. She had her business to get back to. My brother and I had ours.

Thinking it over since, I have come to believe that maybe another rule came to an end along with it. This one was a rule that I had no less devastatingly laid down for myself, and it was this: that I had no right to be happy unless the people I loved—especially my children—were happy too. I have come to believe that that is not true. I believe instead that we all of us have not only the right to be happy no matter what but also a kind of sacred commission to be happy—in the sense of being free to breathe and move, in the sense of being able to bless our own lives, even the sad times of our own lives, because through all our times we can learn and grow, and through all our times, if we keep our ears open, God speaks to us his saving word. Then by drawing on all those times we have had, we can sometimes even speak and live a saving word to the saving of others. I have come to believe that to be happy inside ourselves—to live less and less as the years go by in the dungeon of the Little Ease and more and more in the still chapel where beyond all understanding there is peace—is in the long run the best we can do both for ourselves and for the people closest to us. If we do it right, maybe they can be helped to be a little stronger through our strength, maybe even a little happier through our happiness.

"Rejoice in the Lord, always," Saint Paul wrote to the Philippians. He was in prison when he wrote them, but, inside himself, marvelously unimprisoned. "Again

I will say, Rejoice. Let all men know your forbearance.
The Lord is at hand" (Phil. 4:4–5). Or as my dead father put it, "I know plenty, and it's all good." "That is
the secret I never knew," he also said. It is all good. There
is nothing to worry about. That is the gladdest and most
final of all secrets which I suspect the whole human
family since the world began has glimpsed always in
its holiest dreams.

Is the Lord at hand indeed? Many of us have believed in him for a long time, have also hungered to
believe in him when with part of ourselves we sometimes couldn't believe in much of anything. In the midst
of a suffering world and of our own small suffering, we
have tried to believe in a God of love and power, the
highest power beyond all others. Have we been right?
Is it finally true what we have believed and hungered
to believe? This side of Paradise, who can say with
absolute certainty? Who can say anything that really
matters about anything with absolute certainty? Even
Jesus on his cross asked that hardest of questions.

There are a few lines from a novel called *Thomas
Wingfold*,* that seem to me as honest an answer to that
question as any I happen to have come across lately.
The speaker is a minister named Thomas Wingfold,
and he is describing the years he has spent in the service of Christ and his Kingdom.

> Whatever energies I may or may not have, I know
> one thing for certain: that I could not devote them to

Curate by George MacDonald (New York, George Routledge,
1876, pp. 490–91).

anything else I should think entirely worth doing. Indeed nothing else seems interesting enough, nothing to repay the labor, but the telling of my fellow-men about the one man who is the truth, and to know whom is the life. Even if there be no hereafter, I would live my time believing in a grand thing that ought to be true if it is not. No facts can take the place of truths; and if these be not truths, then is the loftiest part of our nature a waste. Let me hold by the better than the actual, and fall into nothingness off the same precipice with Jesus and John and Paul and a thousand more, who were lovely in their lives, and with their death make even the nothingness into which they have passed like the garden of the Lord. I will go farther, and say I would rather die forevermore believing as Jesus believed, than live forevermore believing as those that deny him.

Is it true, what Jesus believed, this Truth that he died for and lived for? Maybe the only way to know finally this side of falling off that precipice ourselves is to stop speaking and thinking and reading about it so much and to start watching and listening. That is very hard for me to do because I am an addicted speaker, thinker, reader. It is also only during the last few years that I have begun to discover something about what watching and listening involve. I am talking about prayer — prayer not as speaking to God, which in a scattered way I do many times a day because I cannot help doing it, but prayer as being deeply silent, as watching and listening for God to speak.

I have written at length here about the way God speaks through the hieroglyphics of the things that happen to us, and I believe that is true. But I have come to believe more and more that God also speaks through the fathomless quiet of the holy place in the White Tower within us all which is beyond the power of anything that happens to us to touch although many things that happen to us block our access to it, make us forget even that it exists. I believe that this quiet and holy place in us is God's place and that it is what marks us as God's. Even when we have no idea of seeking it, I think various things can make us fleetingly aware of its presence — a work of art, beauty, sometimes sorrow or joy, sometimes just the quality of a moment that apparently has nothing special about it at all like the sound of water over stones in a stream or sitting alone with your feet up at the end of a hard day.

What deadens us most to God's presence within us, I think, is the inner dialogue that we are continuously engaged in with ourselves, the endless chatter of human thought. I suspect that there is nothing more crucial to true spiritual *comfort*, as the huge monk in cloth of gold put it, than being able from time to time to stop that chatter including the chatter of spoken prayer. If we choose to seek the silence of the holy place, or to open ourselves to its seeking, I think there is no surer way than by keeping silent.

God knows I am no good at it, but I keep trying, and once or twice I have been lucky, graced. I have been conscious but not conscious of anything, not even of myself. I have been surrounded by the whiteness of snow. I have heard a stillness that encloses all sounds stilled the way whiteness encloses all colors stilled, the way wordlessness encloses all words stilled. I have sensed the presence of a presence. I have felt a promise promised.

I like to believe that once or twice, at times like those, I have bumbled my way into at least the outermost suburbs of the Truth that can never be told but only come upon, that can never be proved but only lived for and loved. It is the experience that I think the author of the 131st Psalm is trying to describe, and I will let the final word be his.

O Lord, my heart is not lifted up,
    my eyes are not raised too high;
I do not occupy myself with things
    too great and too marvelous for me.
But I have calmed and quieted my soul,
    like a child quieted at its mother's breast,
    like a child that is quieted is my soul.

O Israel, hope in the Lord
    from this time forth and for evermore.

LINCOLN CHRISTIAN COLLEGE AND SEMINARY

THIS BIBLE BELONGS TO

PRESENTED BY

OCCASION

DATE

Precious Moments® Storybook Bible
© 2010 by Thomas Nelson, Inc.

Artwork © 2010 by Precious Moments, Inc.
Licensee, Thomas Nelson, Inc. All Rights Reserved Worldwide.

Stories retold from the International Children's Bible® by
Jennifer Morgan Gerelds

Editorial: Beverly Riggs, Micah Walker, Dana Long

Design and composition: Richmond & Williams, Brentwood, Tennessee

All Rights Reserved
Printed in China
1 2 3 4 5 6 7 8 9 10 – 16 15 14 13 12 11 10

Dedicated to John Burt, the "sucker man,"
who modeled the joy of the Lord for children of all ages.

Children
of Promise

We have such high hopes for our children. We bathe them, feed them, and search for the right clothes. We put them in schools where we believe they will best grow. We treat them with special delights, simply because we long to see the smiles on their faces. We love them. We want the very best for them, and we're willing to make sacrifices to ensure that no good thing is withheld from them. And we wait. We hope. We pray that these children of promise will eventually fulfill their God-given destiny.

But what do we really want for our kids? Is it to be rich? Famous? Athletic? Scholarly? While none of these are wrong in themselves, they all fall short of the purpose and meaning which God intends his children to experience. As much as we love our kids, God loves them more. He wants to give them the very best that there is in this life—and that best is God Himself.

As parents, we have an incredible opportunity—and calling—to introduce our children to God and his Word. To let them know God longs to walk with them all the days of their lives. You can help cultivate this relationship by praying for and with your children, and by reading the truth of God's Word to them. It is the one investment you make as a parent that you can know will pay rich dividends in the end.

The *Precious Moments® Storybook Bible* is so exciting! Yes, it's a beautiful book, filled with all the adorable Precious Moments® characters you and your children have come to love. The illustrations alone will leave your children captivated, waiting to hear what other special stories hide within its pages. But beyond a children's storybook, this precious keepsake retells the stories and truths of the Bible in a way that children can understand. The text is based on the International Children's Bible® translation and presented in a way that little hearts and minds can embrace. As they grow older, they will find the text just as easy to read as it is to hear you read.

They will be entertained, for sure, and educated in Bible truths at the same time. But more than that, as God assures us, they will be changed. They will remember the sweet faces and the truths that they illustrate. God's Word will be hidden in their tiny hearts, and it will grow in them and shine its light through them. Then, when they become parents themselves, they can take this same Bible, open its pastel-painted pages, and pour the love of God into their children too—continuing the rich spiritual heritage that began around the rocking chair in your home. The *Precious Moments*® *Storybook Bible* is a beautiful way to introduce your young ones to a personal relationship with God, and a precious reminder of God's faithfulness that you can lovingly pass down to future generations.

Family Tree

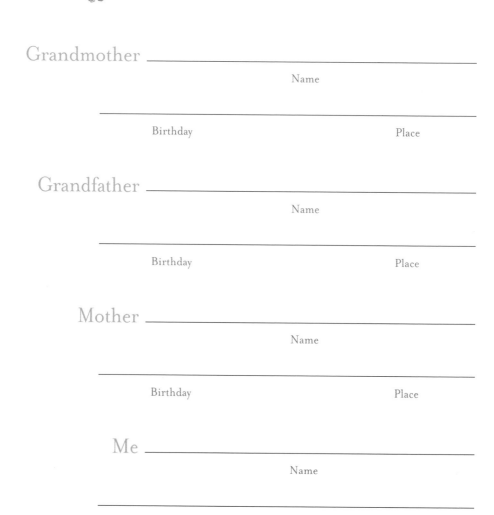

Grandmother _____
Name

_____
Birthday   Place

Grandfather _____
Name

_____
Birthday   Place

Mother _____
Name

_____
Birthday   Place

Me _____
Name

_____
Birthday   Place

Grandmother

_____

Name

_____

Birthday   Place

Grandfather

_____

Name

_____

Birthday   Place

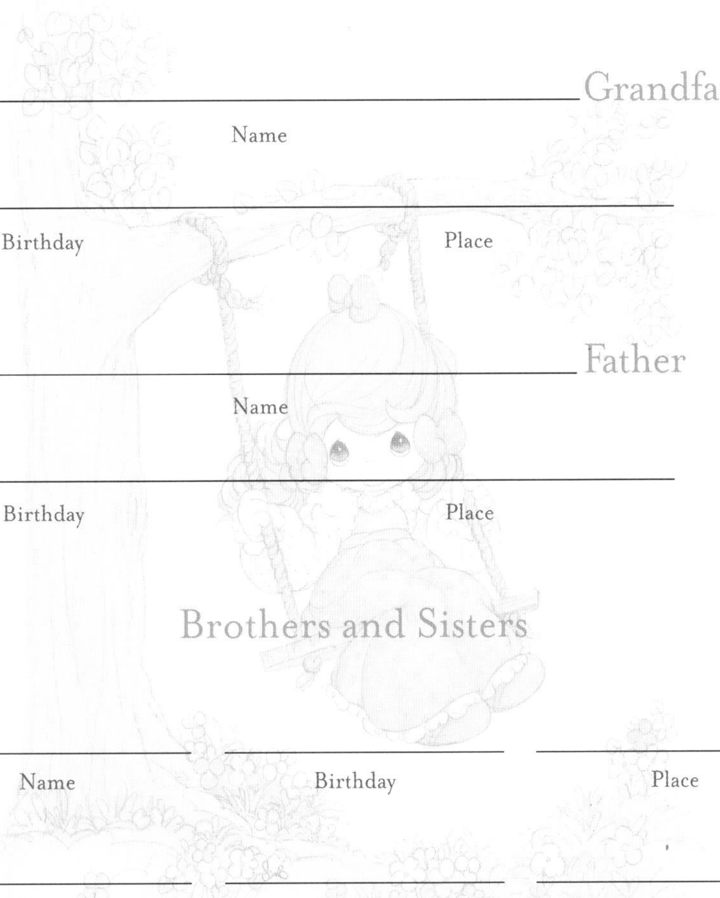

Father

_____

Name

_____

Birthday   Place

Brothers and Sisters

_____

Name   Birthday   Place

_____

Name   Birthday   Place

_____

Name   Birthday   Place

_____

Name   Birthday   Place

Church Record

Special Ceremonies

(Baptism, Dedication, Christening,
First Communion, Confirmation . . .)

Ceremony	Date
Ceremony	Date
Ceremony	Date
Ceremony	Date
Ceremony	Date

Church & Sunday Schools Attended

Church	City	Date
Church	City	Date
Church	City	Date

Vacation Bible Schools

Church	City	Date
Church	City	Date
Church	City	Date

Church Camps

Church	City	Date
Church	City	Date
Church	City	Date

Church Outings

Outing	Event	Date
Outing	Event	Date
Outing	Event	Date

My Favorite Things

Favorite Places _____

_____

Favorite Foods _____

_____

Favorite Pets _____

_____

Favorite Toys _____

_____

Favorite Games/Sports _____

_____

Favorite Songs _____

_____

Table of Contents

Favorite Bible Classics

Words of Praise and Wisdom

Favorite Bible Classics

Creation

Genesis 1–2

In the very beginning, the earth was empty and dark. Suddenly, God said, "Let there be light!"

Bright, shining light streamed from the sky. "That's good!" God smiled. He separated the light from the darkness. Then there was day and night! It was the first day.

Next, God made air to divide the water in two. God named the air "sky."

Then God decided, "It's time for the dry land to appear!" Mountains shot up from the seas.

Beaches glistened in the sun. Rolling hills and plains stretched on for miles.

"And now for the trees and plants," God said. Then he created delicious fruit trees and towering pines. He dotted the land with shrubs and flowers, vines and vegetables. The rich rainbow of colors soaked up the light. It's good!" God said again.

Looking to the skies, God spoke again.
"Shine warmly, sun! Glow brightly, moon!"
And all the stars God made twinkled in the
night sky.

On the fifth day, God added new life!
Suddenly, colorful birds appeared and
flapped their wings for the first time. Then
the waters on the earth began to bubble and

swirl. Fish were swimming everywhere! And all the other sea creatures God made joined in the fun.

But his creation wasn't finished. "Let there be furry bunnies and fast cheetahs!" God said with delight. "Fill the land with wrinkly elephants and tall giraffes. Let the animals play on my earth!" And they did. "That's good too!" God said.

Then the Lord God took dust from the ground and formed man from it. He breathed onto the shape, and it moved! He was alive! "His name is Adam," God said. Then God made Eve from one of Adam's ribs. "I want you to have big families and take care of my creation!" God said. Looking over all he had made, God said this time, "It's very good!"

The Garden of Eden

Genesis 3

A very clever snake slithered up to Eve in the garden. She didn't know it was the devil trying to trick her.

"Did God really say that you can't eat any fruit in the garden?" the snake hissed.

"Oh, no," Eve answered. "We may eat fruit from the garden! We just can't eat or touch the fruit from the tree in the middle of the garden. If we do," she added, "God says we'll die."

"You will not die!" the snake lied. "You'll just learn about good and evil. You'll be just like God!"

Eve looked at the fruit. It was so shiny and colorful! Then she took a bite. "It's delicious! Here, Adam, you try it!" She handed it to him. Adam ate it too.

Suddenly, everything changed. "We need to put some clothes on," Adam and Eve said, as they noticed they were naked. "Let's sew some leaves for clothes." Then they heard God coming. "Let's hide!" they whispered.

"What have you done, Adam?" God asked, even though he knew they had disobeyed.

"It's Eve's fault," Adam answered. "She gave me the fruit."

"But the snake tricked me!" Eve cried.

So God punished the snake, then Eve and Adam.

It was so sad! Adam and Eve had to leave the beautiful garden. But God still loved them deeply. He clothed them with animal skins and found them a new place to live.

Noah and the Ark

Genesis 6–9

Many years had passed since God made the earth. People were everywhere! Sadly, all the people had forgotten about God. They did whatever they wanted. They disobeyed God every day.

But Noah was different. He remembered God and loved him with all of his heart. He obeyed God, even when no one else did.

"Noah," God said one day, "you need to build a very large boat. I'm going to save you and your family. I'll even send two of each kind of animal to put on the boat. But I'm going to destroy everything else with a flood."

Noah obeyed God right away. He followed God's directions carefully. It took a very long time to finish the boat. All the people thought Noah was crazy.

But he wasn't. When he finally finished, God brought animals of every kind to the ark. "Take your family and the animals inside," God said. Then it happened!

Splish. Splash. Fat drops of rain hit the ground. "What's this?" the people cried. But it was too late! Suddenly, rain gushed like a waterfall. Underground springs split, and water shot up, lifting the boat. Only Noah, his family, and the animals inside the ark were safe.

The rain lasted for forty days and nights. After it stopped, it took a very long time for the water to dry up. At last, land appeared. "It's time!" Noah called out. Everyone got off the boat. God had saved them!

Noah made an offering to show God his thanks. "I'll never destroy the earth with a flood again," God said. Then God painted the sky with a beautiful rainbow as a sign of his promise.

Joseph Sold into Slavery

Genesis 37

Jacob had twelve sons. Joseph, though, was his favorite. "Look, Joseph," Jacob said one day. "I have made you a beautiful robe!" Joseph loved it, but the gift made all his brothers very jealous.

Later, Joseph began to have strange dreams. He told his parents and brothers about them. "I had a dream that while we were working in the field, all your bundles of grain bowed down to mine!" In another

dream, Joseph remembered seeing the sun, moon, and eleven stars. "All of them bowed down to me!" he said with excitement. But his brothers just got angrier.

One day, Jacob told Joseph to go find his brothers. They were tending sheep far from home. Joseph gladly obeyed, not knowing what his brothers had planned.

When the brothers saw Joseph coming, they whispered, "Now's our chance to get rid of that dreamer! Let's kill him!" But Reuben stopped them. "Let's just throw him in this dry well, instead."

When Joseph arrived, they tore off his robe and threw him in the well. "I know," said Judah. "Let's sell him to slave traders! Then we can make some money!" Everyone agreed. Soon they had sold Joseph to be a slave in Egypt.

Then, they put goat's blood on Joseph's robe and walked home. They showed it to their father. "My son has been killed by a wild animal!" Jacob sobbed. He didn't know that Joseph would become a successful ruler in Egypt and a faithful man who loved his God.

Moses and the Basket

Exodus 2

God's people had had many children and grandchildren in Egypt. Now there were so many Israelites that the king of Egypt became upset. "Look! The people of Israel are too many and too strong for us to handle!" he said. "Don't let any of their baby boys live," he ordered the Hebrew nurses.

Meanwhile, a family that loved God gave birth to a beautiful baby boy. "I don't want him to die," his mother said. So she made a basket that could float. Then she put baby

Moses inside it and gently set the basket in the Nile River. Miriam, Moses' sister, watched the basket from a distance.

Just a short time later, the basket floated near where the princess of Egypt was taking a bath. "What's that?" she asked her servant girls. "Get that basket for me." They brought it to her, and she discovered the baby inside. "Oh, he's crying!" she exclaimed. "This is one of the Hebrew babies."

Miriam had been watching everything. Quickly, she stepped forward. "I can get a Hebrew mother to nurse him for you," she offered. The princess agreed, and Miriam ran to get her mother.

So Moses grew up in the palace courts, tended by his real family and Egyptian kings and queens.

Crossing the Red Sea

Exodus 14

The people of Egypt had already seen God's anger at their sin. Nine horrible plagues had almost completely destroyed their land. During the tenth plague, the king's own firstborn son died. "Get up and leave my people!" Egypt's king ordered Moses. "Go worship God with all his people, and bless me!" Moses and the Israelites quickly gathered their belongings and left Egypt to follow God.

Moses led the huge crowd of Israelites across the dusty land. God guided them all by a cloud pillar during the day. At night, the cloud became a pillar of fire lighting their way. They were so happy to leave Egypt!

But suddenly, Egypt's king changed his mind. "What have we done? We have lost our slaves!" he roared. "Go after them!" he commanded all the soldiers in his powerful army.

By that time, Moses and God's people were camped at the Red Sea. Soon, they could see Egypt's army racing toward them. "We're going to die!" they cried. But Moses said, "Don't be afraid! Stand still and see the Lord save you today!"

Then Moses lifted his staff toward the Red Sea. Instantly, the deep waters cracked and pulled apart! A dry path stretched in front of them. All God's people crossed through the walls of water to the land on the other side.

Egypt's soldiers kept charging. Soldiers, horses, and chariots thundered onto the dry path. When all the Israelites were safely on shore, Moses held out his hand over the water. Crash! The walls of water smashed together and drowned the entire Egyptian army. God saved his people!

God's Commands

Exodus 19–20

*T*hree months had passed since Israel had left Egypt. God gathered his people at the base of a very tall mountain. Then God called to Moses. "Come up here to meet with me," he said. So Moses left the people of God and climbed Mount Sinai to talk with God.

"Tell this to the people of Israel," God instructed Moses. "Everyone has seen how I saved you from the Egyptians. So now obey me and be my special people. You will be different from everyone else because you will belong to me, and I will be your God."

So Moses climbed down the mountain and told the people what God had said. "We will do everything he has said," the people promised. So Moses returned to God on the mountain.

Suddenly, thunder and lightning flashed and a very thick cloud covered the top of the mountain. A loud trumpet blasted and the mountain shook wildly. The Lord was meeting with Moses!

"I am the Lord your God. Do not worship fake gods. Only worship me," God commanded. "Do not make any idols, and do not disrespect my name by saying it without thinking," he continued.

"Remember that the Sabbath is a day of rest. Don't tell lies about your neighbor. And do not want to take your neighbor's belongings."

All the people were afraid when they heard the thunder and the trumpet. "Speak to us yourself, Moses. Then we will listen," they pleaded. "But don't let God speak to us, or we will die." So Moses explained to them all that God had commanded.

The People's Sin

Exodus 31–32

God wanted his people to be different! Since they belonged to God, he wanted them to be perfect like him. He also wanted to meet with them. So he told them how to build a special tent called the Tent of Meeting. He would meet with the priests there to tell them what he wanted the people to know.

Then God wrote his rules down on two stone tablets. He gave them to Moses. But then something bad happened while Moses was on the mountain with God.

"Go down from this mountain," God suddenly told Moses. "Your people are doing very evil things!"

Moses quickly climbed down the mountain with Joshua, his helper. Together, they heard the noise of a great big party. Then they found out why the people were celebrating.

While Moses was away, the people had gotten tired of waiting. "Aaron, we don't know what happened to Moses, so make us gods who will lead us!" they insisted. Aaron agreed, and gathered their gold jewelry. Then he melted it and shaped the gold into the form of a calf. The people loved it!

They danced wildly and worshiped the idol. They broke all of God's commands.

When Moses saw it, he was so angry! He threw his stone tablets on the ground and shattered them. Then he melted the idol, crushed it to powder, put it in water, and made the Israelites drink it.

The next day, Moses told the people, "You have sinned terribly. But now I will go to the Lord and ask him to forgive you."

David and Goliath

1 Samuel 17

The powerful Philistine army lined the hill. The Israelite army lined up on another hill, facing the Philistines. Only a small valley separated the soldiers. Every day, the Philistines sent their very best soldier named Goliath to make fun of the Israelites. He was nine-foot-four-inches tall, he carried very heavy armor and a spear, and he made fun of Israel's God. "Send someone to fight me!" he ordered. "If he can fight and kill me, we will become your servants. But if I defeat and kill him, you will become our servants!" All the Israelites were afraid. No one wanted to fight Goliath.

Meanwhile, in the city of Bethlehem, a young boy named David was taking care of his sheep. Jesse, his father, sent him to check on his brothers who were in the army.

When David arrived at the camp, he heard Goliath. "Why does he think he can say bad things about our God?" David demanded to know. "I will go and fight this Philistine!" David said. He knew God would take care of him.

King Saul heard about David and sent for him. "You can't fight that mean soldier! You're only a boy. Goliath is a mighty warrior!"

David answered, "The Lord will fight for me!" Instead of the king's armor, David chose five smooth stones from a stream and a sling. Then he went to meet Goliath.

Goliath saw David coming. The giant soldier began making fun of David, too. But David shouted back, "You come to me using a sword and spear. But I come to you in the name of the Lord!"

Then David ran fast toward Goliath and flung the rock from his sling. The stone sank deeply into Goliath's forehead and he fell down dead. Israel's army cheered in triumph and chased the Philistine army away.

Jesus Visits the Temple

Luke 2

*E*very year Jesus' parents went to Jerusalem for the Passover Feast. When Jesus was 12 years old, they went to the feast as they always did. When it was over, they started toward home.

After traveling a full day, Mary asked Joseph, "Where is Jesus?" They began to ask friends and relatives. "We haven't seen him," they all said. Mary and Joseph were worried. "We must go back to Jerusalem and look for him there," they decided.

Mary and Joseph searched Jerusalem for three days. At last, they found Jesus in the Temple talking with the priests and teachers. He was asking them questions and listening to them. "This boy has amazing understanding and wise answers!" the leaders said.

"Son, why did you do this to us?" Mary asked Jesus. "Your father and I were very worried about you. We have been looking for you!"

Jesus answered, "Why did you have to look for me? You should have known that I must be where my Father's work is!" Mary and Joseph did not understand what Jesus meant, but they were very happy to find him. "Let's go home now," they said. Jesus gladly obeyed.

At home, Jesus continued to learn more and more and to grow bigger and stronger. People liked him, and he pleased God.

Sermon on the Hill

Matthew 5

Crowds of people followed Jesus. They all wanted to hear what he had to say. So he went up on a hill with his followers to teach them. He said:

"Everyone who knows they need God is happy because the kingdom of heaven belongs to them.

"Those who are sad are happy because God will comfort them.

"Those who are humble are happy because the earth will belong to them.

"Those who really want to do right are happy because God will give them everything they need.

"Those who show kindness to others are happy because kindness will be given them.

"Those who are pure in their thinking are happy because they will be with God.

"Those who work to bring peace are happy. God will call them his sons.

"And those who are treated badly for doing good are happy because the kingdom of heaven belongs to them."

Then Jesus explained that people will say bad things about his followers. "They will lie and say evil things because you follow me," Jesus

warned. "But when they do, rejoice and be glad! You have a great reward waiting for you in heaven."

Then Jesus taught his people that they are the salt of the earth and the light to the world. "Live so that others will see the good things you do. Live so that they will praise your Father in heaven," Jesus encouraged them.

Jesus Feeds the 5,000 and Walks on Water

Matthew 14

All day, Jesus taught the people and healed the sick. At last, it was time for dinner. Everybody was hungry. "Send the people to town so they can buy some food," Jesus' followers said. But Jesus answered, "You give them some food to eat."

"But, we don't have enough food!" they argued. "We have only five loaves of bread and two fish."

Jesus told everybody to sit down. Then he took what little food they had and prayed. "Thank you, Father, for this food," he said. Then he put the food into baskets and had his followers pass them around. Women and children, along with 5,000 men, sat on the ground, and they all took what they needed.

Soon, everyone said, "I'm full!" When the followers gathered the baskets, they found twelve still filled with leftover food!

After dinner, it was time to go. Jesus sent his followers ahead of him by boat.

During the night, a strong wind blew over the lake and kicked up very high waves. Suddenly, the followers saw a man walking on the water! "It's a ghost!" they cried.

But Jesus said, "It is I! Don't be afraid."

Peter answered, "If it's you, tell me to come to you on the water."

"Come," Jesus welcomed him.

Peter hopped out of the boat and walked on the water to Jesus. But when he saw the wind and waves, he became afraid and started to sink. "Lord, save me!" Peter cried. Jesus grabbed Peter and brought him to the boat.

"Your faith is small," Jesus gently corrected him. "Why did you stop believing?"

Then the wind and waves grew calm.

Jesus Is Killed on a Cross
John 19–20

No matter what Pilate said, the people wanted to kill Jesus. "Take Jesus away and whip him," Pilate ordered his soldiers. They eagerly obeyed. Then they made a crown out of thorny branches and pushed it on his head. They draped a purple robe over his shoulders and made fun of him. "Hail, king of the Jews!" they laughed. They spit on him and hit him.

The religious leaders and crowd shouted, "Take him away! Kill him on a cross!" Then Pilate ordered Jesus to be killed.

Jesus stumbled to Golgotha. The cross he carried was very heavy. There, they nailed his hands and feet to the wood. Above his head, they nailed a sign that read, "JESUS OF NAZARETH, KING OF THE JEWS."

As Jesus hung on the cross, the soldiers decided to play a game. "Whoever wins gets to keep Jesus' clothes," they said. Everything happened just like the Bible said it would.

At last, Jesus cried out, "It is finished!" Then he bowed his head and died.

To make sure he was dead, the soldiers pierced

Jesus' side with a spear. They didn't break any of his bones.

Later, Joseph of Arimathea asked Pilate, "May I take Jesus' body down for burial?" Pilate said yes. Joseph and Nicodemus wrapped Jesus' body in linen cloth with many spices and laid his body in a new tomb.

The Empty Tomb

John 20–21

It was the first day of the week. Light from the early morning sun had just begun to shine. Mary Magdalene was already awake. She wanted to go visit Jesus' tomb as soon as possible. But when she arrived, she became scared. "The stone has been moved away!" she gasped. Then she ran as fast as she could to tell the other followers. "They have taken the Lord out of the tomb. We don't know where they've put him!"

Peter and another follower ran back to the tomb to see for themselves. They went inside and saw the clothes that had wrapped Jesus' body. *But where was Jesus?* they wondered. Then they hurried back to tell the others.

Meanwhile, Mary stood outside the tomb crying. Suddenly, she saw two angels sitting where Jesus' body had been. "Why are you crying?" they asked her. "They have taken away my Lord," she sobbed. As she turned around, she saw another man that she thought was the gardener.

He asked her, "Woman, why are you crying? Who are you looking for?" She answered him, "Did you take him away, sir? Tell me where you put him, and I will go get him."

Then Jesus said, "Mary!" Immediately, Mary knew who he was. "Rabboni!" she rejoiced. (This means Teacher.) Jesus said, "Go back to my brothers and tell them this: 'I am going back to my Father and your Father, to my God and your God.'"

So Mary Magdalene ran back to tell Jesus' followers the incredible news. "I saw the Lord!" she shouted. And then she told them everything Jesus said.

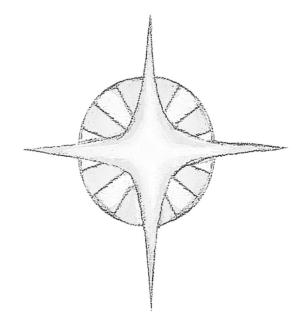

Jesus Goes Back to Heaven

Luke 24

Many people had seen Jesus after he came back to life. Two men had actually walked and talked with Jesus on the road to Emmaus. They went to tell his other followers all that they had seen and heard. While everyone was standing around talking about it, Jesus himself appeared among them.

"Peace be with you," he announced. His followers were terrified! *Is this a ghost?* they wondered. But Jesus calmed them. "Why are you afraid? Why do you think I'm not real?" he asked as he reached toward them. "Look at my hands and feet. It's me! Touch me. You can see that I have a living body; a ghost does not have a body like this."

The followers were amazed and very happy. Then Jesus reminded them about the Scriptures. Even from long ago, the messages explained how Jesus would come to save lost sinners. Then Jesus helped them understand.

"Listen! My Father has promised to send you the Holy Spirit. He will help you,"

Jesus said. "Stay in Jerusalem until you have received that power from heaven."

Then Jesus led his followers out of Jerusalem. Outside the city, he raised his hands and blessed them. As he spoke, he was carried into heaven. "Praise Jesus, the Son of God!" his followers worshiped. After awhile, they went back to Jerusalem, still excited about everything God had done. They stayed in the temple all the time and worshiped God.

Words of Praise and Wisdom

Your Name Is Wonderful

Psalm 8:1-8

Lord, you are our Master! Your name is the most wonderful of all! The heavens shout your praise. You have taught children and even babies to sing about how great you are!

I look at the heavens, which you made with your hands. I see the moon and stars, which you created. They seem so big and important, but we are so small.

Why are people important to you? Why do you take care of us?

Though we are small, you have made us very special. You put your people in charge of everything you made! Your people rule over all the fluffy sheep and grazing cows, all the powerful lions and strong bears. You've put us in charge of all the majestic eagles and colorful parrots, and even the mighty sharks and whales! Our power comes from you, and you rule over us.

Lord our Master, your name is the most wonderful name in all the earth!

The Lord Takes Care of His People

Psalm 16:1–9, 11

*P*rotect me, God, because I trust in you. I said to the Lord, "You are my Lord. Every good thing I have comes from you."

I love to be with other people who serve and love you, God. But some people have turned from you. They worship fake idols. I will never follow them.

No, the Lord is all I need. He takes care of me. You have made my life beautiful.

Praise your name, Lord! You guide me through the day; even at night you keep on leading me. I will always keep you in front of me so that I know where to go. I will not be hurt. So I'm happy, and I am glad! Even my body has hope.

You will teach me God's way to live. Being with you fills me with so much joy! Being right beside you brings me more happiness than anything else.

The Lord Is My Shepherd

Psalm 23:1-6

The Lord is my shepherd. He gives me everything I need! When I'm tired, he takes me to beautiful, green grass for rest. He takes me to drink from cool, calm waters. He gives me strength for the day. Because he is good, he leads me on the right paths. Even if I walk through a very dark valley, I will not be afraid because you are with me. You protect me with your shepherd's rod and staff.

You prepare a meal for me in front of my enemies. They see how good you are to me. You pour oil on my head. You give me more than I can hold. I can never outlive your goodness and love to me. And I will live in the Lord's house forever!

Telling the Truth

Psalm 32:1-11

When God forgives our sin, we are so happy! What a blessing that God can take our guilt away! When we are forgiven, we are perfect before God.

But sometimes I tried to hide my sin. It made me feel weak deep inside me. I worried all day long. My strength was gone as in the summer heat.

Then I told you what I did wrong. I quit hiding my sin, and I turned to you. I said,

"I will confess my sins to the Lord." And you forgave me!

We should all pray to you right away, while there is time. When troubles rise like a flood, I will not get hurt. I hide in you because you protect me. You fill me with happy songs about how you saved me.

The Lord says, "I will make you wise. I will show you where to go. I will guide you and watch over you. Don't be like a horse or donkey. They don't understand. They must be led with bits and reins, or they will not come near you."

People who turn from God run into a lot of trouble, but the Lord's love covers those who trust him. Everyone, sing and be happy in the Lord!

Wishing to Be Near God

Psalm 63:1–8

God, you are my God. I want to follow you! I am like a person who travels in a hot, dry desert. I am so thirsty for you!

I have seen you with my own eyes in your beautiful Temple. You are so strong and full of glory! Your love is better than anything else in life. I will tell how great you are as long as I live! When I pray to you, I will lift up my hands. I know good will come from you. I will be full of your goodness, as if I had just eaten the very best meal. I will use the mouth you gave me to sing praises to you.

While I'm lying in bed, I remember you and think about you through the night. You help me! Because you protect me, I sing with joy. Your strong hand supports me, so I will always stay by your side!

Lord, Teach Me Your Rules

Psalm 119:1-2, 9-20, 24

People who live pure lives and keep God's rules are the happiest of all. They follow the Lord and ask him for help!

How can a young person live a life that makes God happy? He can do it by obeying God's word! God, I want to obey you with my whole heart. Please help me to do what's right. I have put your words in my heart so that I won't forget them and sin against you.

Lord, you should be praised. Teach me what you want. Then I'll tell other people about all your right ways. I enjoy living by your rules as much as some people enjoy a lot of money. I think about your orders and study your ways. Because I enjoy your words so much, I will not forget them.

Keep being good to me so that I can obey you. Please open my eyes so that I can see how wonderful your teachings truly are! This earth is not my home. I want to study and know your ways. Please don't hide them from me!

I delight in your rules. They're the best teachings for my life!

The Word of God

Psalm 119:73, 76-77, 89-90, 105, 111-112, 114, 117, 127

You created me with your own hands, so you can help me understand you. Teach me so that I can learn your ways.

I love to serve you. You promised to comfort me with your love. Please show kindness to me so that I may live a good life. How I love your teachings!

Lord, your word never ends! It stays true forever in heaven. You never stop being

friends with your people. You made the earth, and it still stands.

Your word lights my way like a bright and shining lamp.

I will follow your rules forever. They make me happy! I will try to always do what you have asked for as long as I live.

You protect me like a shield, so I hide myself in you.

Help me, and I will be saved. I will always respect your rules.

I love your commands more than the purest gold.

Protection and Guidance

Psalm 121:1-8

The hills do not protect me. So where does my help come from? It comes from the Lord! He made heaven and earth.

He will not let you be defeated. The Lord always guards you. He never sleeps or even rests! The Lord protects you as the shade protects you from the sun. The sun cannot hurt you during the day. And the moon cannot hurt you at night.

The Lord will guard your life from all dangers. He will protect you in all that you do—both now and forever.

Praise
the Lord
Psalm 150:1-6

*P*raise the Lord!

Praise God in his Temple. Worship him in his mighty heaven. How strong and great is our God!

Sound the trumpets. Pluck the harps and lyres. Dance and shake the tambourine. Play the flute. Fill the air with the sound of stringed instruments. Praise him with loud, crashing cymbals. Let everything that breathes praise the Lord!

Praise the Lord!

The Wise Words of Solomon

Proverbs 1:1-9, 15

David's son, Solomon, became Israel's king. These are his wise words:

The smart person listens to words of wisdom. By them, you learn how to obey and understand God's rules. They teach you what is honest, fair, and right. They help you to think the right way, even if you don't know everything. Smart people listen to them and keep on learning.

They learn how to understand the words and riddles of wise men.

Being wise starts with loving and obeying the Lord. Only foolish people hate following his ways.

My child, listen to what your mother and father teach you. Their instruction will make your life beautiful, like a gold necklace or fragrant flowers in your hair.

Do not follow sinners who tell you to go the wrong way. Do not do what they do!

The Rewards of Wisdom

Proverbs 2:1-12

My child, believe and remember what I say! Listen to my wise words. Do everything you can to understand. Call out to God for wisdom. Beg for understanding. Search for it like a hidden treasure. When you do, you will start to understand how great the Lord is.

As you learn respect, you will begin to know God. Only the Lord gives wisdom and understanding. He gladly gives it to those who are honest. Like a shield he protects the people

who haven't done wrong and those who stay close friends with God.

Then you will understand what is honest and fair and right. You'll know what to do. Your good sense will protect you and keep you from doing evil. It will save you from people who speak lies.

Remember the Lord

Proverbs 3:1-8

My child, don't forget my teaching. Keep thinking about what I've said. Then you'll live a long time and your life will be very good.

Don't ever stop being kind and truthful. Let truth and kindness fill everything you do. Write them on your mind like a list on a piece of paper. Then others will think well of you, and God will be happy.

Trust the Lord with all of your heart. Even if it doesn't make sense to you, trust God's words anyway. Remember the Lord in everything you do, and he will tell you where to go.

Don't do what you think is smart. Trust God instead, and do what he tells you. Then you will have a healthy body and strong bones.

Train Up a Child

Proverbs 22:1-4, 6

It is better to be known for your goodness than it is to have a lot of money. It's better for people to think well of you than to own many things.

Rich people and poor people are really the same. God made them all!

When a wise person sees danger coming, he gets out of the way. Foolish people keep going and get into trouble.

Don't be proud. Respect the Lord and he will bring you all that you need in life.

Teach a child how to live God's way when he is young. As he grows up, he will remember what he learned. He will continue to follow God.

A Time for Everything

Ecclesiastes 3:1-8

There is a right time for everything. Everything on earth has its special season. Every day someone is born and someone dies. We plant in the right season, and clear the fields after the food has been picked. At times, we hunt for food. At other times, we help heal those who are hurt. Sometimes we must tear things down before we can build something stronger and better.

Sometimes it is best to cry. But laughing at the right time can be just what is needed.

It is okay to be sad sometimes. When you are happy, it's time to celebrate! There is a time to throw away stones and a time to gather them. Hug someone when the time is right. But don't hug them longer than they want.

Search hard when you lose something, but know when it's time to give up looking. Keep a few special things, but learn to throw the others away. Sometimes it's best to rip things apart. At other times, sew them together.

Be silent when you need to listen. Then speak when the time is right. It is always time to love what is good. Always hate what is evil. Get ready when it's time for war. God will later bring times of peace.

Friends and Family Give Strength

Ecclesiastes 4:9–12

It is much easier to get work done when two people work together. If one person falls and gets hurt, the other person can help him get up. But if he is alone when he falls, no one can help him. It is easier to keep warm when two people are together. When you're all alone, it's hard to stay warm in the cold.

An enemy might be able to hurt someone who is alone. But when people come together, they can protect themselves. A rope made of three strands wrapped together is strong. It's very hard to break.

The King of Peace Is Coming

Isaiah 11:1-7, 9-10

A new king is coming from Jesse's family. He will grow like a branch that grows from an old stump. God's Spirit will fill this king and give him the power to know and obey God perfectly. He will lead God's people in the right way. The Spirit will teach him to know and respect the Lord. He will gladly obey what God says. He will not judge other people by what they look like on the outside.

He will always do what's right. With a word he will destroy evil people, and he will rule with goodness and right judgment.

Even wild animals will grow tame. Wolves will rest with sheep, and leopards will lie calmly with goats. All the animals will eat together in peace. And a little child will lead them.

No one will hurt another anymore because all of creation will know God.

Then the king from Jesse's family will draw people to his home. The place where he lives will shine with his glory!

More
Stories of the
Faith

We Will Serve the Lord

Joshua 24:1–15

Joshua had an important message from God for the people of Israel. Each of the 12 tribes sent a leader to the city of Shechem to hear what God had to say.

"A long time ago, your ancestors worshiped fake gods," God said through Joshua. "But I, the Lord, took Abraham out of that land and I led him to Canaan. I gave Abraham many children through his son Isaac. Over time, his large family became slaves in Israel.

"I chose Moses and Aaron to free you from the Egyptians. When I brought you out of Egypt, their soldiers chased my people on chariots. When Israel cried out for help, I parted the sea so they could walk through safely. But when the Egyptians passed through, I covered their army with water.

"Then I brought you to the land I wanted to give you. I drove out the bad people who lived there to make room for you."

Then Joshua said, "Now you have heard from the Lord. You need to serve him with all of your heart. Today you must decide who you

will serve," he said. "You can serve the same fake gods that our ancestors and these people here worship if you want. But as for me and my family, we will serve the Lord!"

Everyone in Israel agreed with Joshua. "No! We will never stop following the Lord!" they cried.

Daniel in the Lions' Den

Daniel 6:4-23

King Darius loved Daniel because he was a good servant who always did what was right. He also loved God. But Darius's other leaders hated Daniel. They wanted to get rid of him. So Daniel's enemies came up with a plan to trick the king into killing Daniel.

"King Darius, live forever!" they said as they came before his throne. "All of your wise leaders have agreed that you should order a new law," they said. "For the next 30 days, no one should pray to any god or man except you. Anyone who doesn't obey will be thrown into the lions' den!"

So King Darius wrote the new law. Daniel heard about it, but he didn't obey the king. He obeyed God instead. Daniel kept right on praying to God every day, by his window, just like always.

It wasn't hard for Daniel's enemies to catch him. They found him in his upstairs room praying in front of the open windows. They brought him before King Darius.

"King Darius, Daniel is not obeying you. He still prays to his God three times every day," they reported. King Darius became very upset. *Isn't there some way to save Daniel?* he wondered. But the law had already been written.

So the soldiers threw Daniel into the lions' den. King Darius cried, "May the God you serve all the time save you!"

Early the next morning, King Darius hurried back to the lions' den and called out, "Daniel, servant of the living God! Has your God been able to save you from the lions?"

Daniel answered, "My God sent his angel to close the lions' mouths. They have not hurt me!"

Darius was so happy! He quickly freed Daniel. Then he threw his enemies into the den of lions.

Jonah Runs from God

Jonah 1:1—2:10

Long ago, the Lord spoke to Jonah. He said, "I want you to travel to the great city of Nineveh. The people there do many bad things and I want you to preach against it."

But Jonah ran away from the Lord and went to the city of Joppa instead. He found a ship going to a city called Tarshish. He paid the crew to let him ride on the ship, thinking he could escape the Lord.

But the Lord sent a storm on the sea and made it very rough. The ship was in danger of breaking apart. All the sailors were afraid it would sink, so they started throwing things off to make the boat lighter. They prayed to their gods for help.

Jonah was asleep on the ship when the captain came and said, "Why are you sleeping? Get up and pray to your God so maybe he will save us!"

Then all the sailors threw lots to find out who was causing the troubles they were having on the sea. It was determined that their trouble had come because of Jonah. Jonah said, "I know it's my fault that the storm has come upon us. Throw me into the sea; then the waters will calm down." So the men picked him up and threw him into the sea. Suddenly, the

water became calm. All the men on the boat feared Jonah's God even more.

Then the Lord caused a very big fish to swallow Jonah. Jonah stayed three days and three nights in the big fish's huge, smelly stomach. While he was there, he prayed to the Lord his God. Jonah said:

"I was in danger, so I called to you and you answered. I was about to die, and you heard me and saved me. You threw me into the sea, and the waters were all around me. But you saved me from death! Lord, I praise you and thank you! Thank you for saving me! I will keep all my promises to you, Lord."

Then the Lord spoke to the big fish. The fish spit Jonah out onto the dry land!

Jesus' Birth and the Wise Men's Visit

Matthew 1:18-24; 2:1-12

Mary was planning to marry Joseph. Suddenly, an angel appeared in her house! "Don't be afraid, Mary, because God is pleased with you!" the angel said. Then he told her that she was going to have a baby. "It will be God's own Son, born through the power of the Holy Spirit," he said.

Surprised, Mary answered, "I am the Lord's servant. Let this happen to me as you say!" Then the angel left.

At first, Joseph was upset when Mary told him the news. But God sent an angel at night to explain God's plan to Joseph. So they married and traveled to Bethlehem, where she gave birth to Jesus.

A short time later, wise men from the east journeyed to Jerusalem to find the special baby. They came to King Herod first and asked, "Where is the baby who was born to be the king of the Jews? We saw his star in the east," they explained. "We came to worship him."

News of a new king bothered King Herod. He told the wise men, "Go and look

carefully to find the child. When you find him, come tell me so I can worship him too." Secretly, Herod planned to kill the new king.

The star continued to lead the wise men straight to Jesus in Bethlehem. When they found him, they were so happy! Bowing before Jesus, they brought him treasures of gold, frankincense, and myrrh. But God warned them not to return to Herod. So the wise men went home another way.

The Light of the World

John 3:1-6, 9-16, 19-21

It was nighttime when Nicodemus came to Jesus. As a Pharisee, he was an important Jewish leader. But he wanted to hear more about what Jesus had to say.

Jesus told him, "I tell you the truth. Unless one is born again, he cannot be in God's kingdom."

Nicodemus was very confused. "How can anyone be born twice?" he asked. So Jesus explained, "He must be born from water and the Spirit." Then Jesus taught Nicodemus

about how all the Scriptures told of Jesus' coming. "The Son of Man must be lifted up on a cross, just like Moses lifted up the snake on the pole in the desert and saved the people," Jesus said. "God loved the world so much that he sent his only Son. Whoever believes in him will not be lost, but will have eternal life."

Then Jesus explained to Nicodemus why some people would not believe him. "I am the Light from God that has come into the world. But some people did not want the light," Jesus told him. "They wanted darkness because the light showed all their bad deeds. But the person who follows the true way loves the light."

Jesus Teaches the People

Matthew 6:7-21, 25, 33

Jesus explained to the people what obedience to God looks like. "Don't be like those people who don't know God but pray to him anyway. They may use big words and sound important, but they don't mean anything," Jesus warned them. "Your Father knows what you need before you even ask him. So when you pray, say:

"Father in heaven, your name is perfect. Please set up your kingdom here on earth like you have in heaven. Give us the food we need each day and forgive us for our sins. We will forgive people who hurt us too. Do not cause us to be tested, but protect us from the Evil One."

Then Jesus showed the difference between people who pretend to know God and real believers. "Don't try to get people to notice you when you fast or pray. Keep it a secret between you and God, and he will reward you. Remember that heavenly treasures are worth a lot more than anything on earth. Moths, rust, and thieves ruin things here, but heavenly riches last forever."

Then Jesus taught them about trust. "Don't worry and say, 'What will we eat?' or 'What will we drink?' or 'What will we wear?' All the people who don't know God worry about these things. But your Father knows what you need, and he will take care of you," Jesus reminded them. "What you should want most is God's kingdom and doing what God wants. He'll give you everything else you need."

The Story About Planting Seed

Matthew 13:3-8, 19-23

Jesus often used stories to help the people understand heavenly ideas. Once he told a story about a man who went out to plant some seed.

Some seed fell by the road, but they were quickly eaten by birds. Some fell on rocky ground and grew into plants quickly. But their roots were short, and the plants withered in the hot sun. Some seed fell among weeds. Though they grew, they were soon choked out

by the weeds. At last, the rest of the seed fell on good ground. They grew strong and tall and produced a large crop.

"So listen to the meaning of that story about the farmer," Jesus said. "The seed that fell by the road is like someone who hears God's Word but doesn't understand it. Then the Evil One comes and takes it away. The seed that fell on rocky ground is like someone who listens to God at first and is happy about it. But when hard times come, he stops believing God. The seed that fell among the thorny weeds is like a person who hears the teaching at first. But soon he lets the problems in this life and the love of money stop that truth from growing. But the seed that fell on good ground is like the person who hears God's words and understands them. He grows to become strong in Jesus and produces fruit."

Jesus Heals and Teaches

Luke 13:10-17; 15:1-7

Jesus loved to teach and to help people. One day he was teaching in the synagogue. A synagogue is similar to a church where people go to worship and learn. There was a woman there who was crippled. Her back was bent, and she could not stand up straight. When Jesus saw her, he said, "Woman, stand up. Your sickness has left you!" He put his hands on her, and instantly she could stand. She was so happy that she began praising God.

But the leader of the synagogue was angry because Jesus had healed her on the Sabbath day. (In those days you were not supposed to do any work on the seventh day, or the Sabbath day.)

Jesus told the synagogue leader that he was being unfair, and he was wrong. He explained, "You untie your work animals and lead them to drink water every day, even on the Sabbath. This woman whom I healed is our Jewish sister. Surely it is not wrong to heal her on a Sabbath day!" When Jesus said this, all the men who were criticizing him were ashamed. All the other people were happy for the wonderful things Jesus was doing.

Another time Jesus told a story to some teachers and other people who were watching

and listening to him. He said, "What if a man had 100 sheep, and one of them wandered off and got lost? That man would leave all the other 99 sheep to go look for his one lost sheep. He would search until he found it. Then when he finally found it, he would be so happy! He would pick up the sheep and carry it home. He would tell his friends and neighbors so they could be happy that he found his lost sheep too. I tell you that it is the same way in heaven when one sinner changes his heart. There is so much happiness and rejoicing that one lost sinner has come to God!"

A Son Comes Home

Luke 15:11-32

Jesus told the story of a man who had two sons. The younger son wanted fun and adventure, so he asked his father for his share of the property. The father divided up the property between his two sons. The younger son took all that was his and left home. He traveled far away to another country. He was foolish and wasted all his money on things that were not good for him. Before he knew it, he had spent all his money.

Then the land got very dry. There was no rain and all the crops died. There was no food to eat. The son was so hungry! He needed money to buy food. But he had wasted all the money he had. So he got a job feeding pigs. He was so hungry that he was even willing to eat the same food the pigs had to eat. But still no one would give him anything.

So he decided that he would just go home and tell his father that he was sorry. Maybe his dad would let him at least be a servant. The servants had enough food to eat. *I will go home and apologize,* he thought.

While the son was still a long way from the house, his father saw him coming. He felt sorry for his son. The father ran to him with wide-open arms. He hugged him and kissed

him and held him tight. Then the father
wanted to have a feast to celebrate his son's
homecoming. He told the servants to bring
food and gifts for the party. "My son was dead,
but now he is alive again! He was lost, but now
he is found!" So they all began to celebrate.

But the older son was still in the field. When he came home, he saw the party and asked one of his father's servants, "What's going on here? Why all this celebrating?" The servant told him about the younger son coming safely home. The older son was angry because he had worked so hard for his father for many years, and the younger son had wasted everything his father had given him. But the father said to him, "Son, you are always with me, and all I have is yours. But we are happy that your brother who was lost is now found!"

Jesus Teaches About Entering the Kingdom of God

Mark 10:13-27

The followers were upset. Many people had brought their children to Jesus so he could touch them. "Stop bringing your children!" the followers said angrily. "Jesus is too busy."

But Jesus said, "Don't stop the children from coming to me. The kingdom of God belongs to people who are like these little children." Then Jesus gathered the children into his arms and blessed them.

As Jesus turned to leave, a man knelt down before him. "Good teacher, what must I do to get the life that never ends?" he asked.

Jesus answered, "You must know God's commands and keep them." Then the man replied, "Teacher, I have obeyed all of God's commands since I was a boy!"

Jesus looked into his eyes. "There is still one more thing you need to do. Go and sell everything you have, and give the money to the poor. You will have a reward in heaven. Then come and follow me."

Full of sadness, the man got up and walked away. He was a very rich man, and he did not want to lose his money—not even for Jesus.

Jesus looked at his followers and said, "It is very hard for a rich person to enter the kingdom of God. It would be easier for a camel to go through the eye of a needle!"

Amazed, his followers asked, "Then who can be saved?"

Jesus answered, "This is something men cannot do. But God can do all things."

Jesus Appears to Thomas

John 20:19-29

Jesus' followers stayed close to one another inside a special locked room. They were afraid that the same people who killed Jesus would come hurt them. Suddenly, Jesus came and stood among them! "Peace be with you!" he greeted them. Then he showed them his hands and his side. They were so happy! Jesus was alive!

Thomas was not with the other followers when Jesus appeared. When his friends ran to tell him the incredible news, Thomas

thought they were lying. "I will not believe it until I put my finger where the nails were in his hands and where the spear pierced his side," Thomas answered.

A week later the followers were in the house again. This time Thomas was with them. Again, the door was locked, but Jesus suddenly appeared inside the room with them. "Peace be with you!" Jesus announced. Then he looked at Thomas. "Come here, Thomas," Jesus called to him. "Put your finger here. Look at my hands. Put your hand here in my side. Stop doubting and believe!"

Thomas cried out, "My Lord and my God!"

Jesus answered, "You believe because you see me. Those who believe without seeing me will be truly happy!"

God's Love

1 Corinthians 13:1-8

Imagine if I could speak every language in the world and even in heaven. It may make me sound special and important. But if I don't have love, then my words are just noise, like a loud bell or ringing cymbal.

Or what if I knew all the secrets of God? Or what if I was the smartest person around; or maybe I had so much faith that I could even move mountains. Wouldn't that make me important? No, if I have all these things but don't have love, I am nothing.

So maybe I give everything to the poor and even give up my life. Is that the best thing

I can do? No, I get nothing by doing even these things if I don't have love.

What is love? It is patient and kind, waiting for others and helping to meet their needs. Love is not jealous, wanting what others have. It does not brag about what it does have.

It is not proud, because everything comes from God. Love is not rude, for it considers others as more important. And it does not become angry easily or remember wrongs done against it, because it is quick to forgive. Love is not happy with evil, but it is happy with the truth.

Love patiently accepts life the way it is, trusting God to do what is best. It always hopes and never gives up, because God is faithful.

Love never ends.

The Full Armor of God

Ephesians 6: 10-18

The Bible tells us about the armor of God. We are to be strong in the Lord—he has great power! We are to wear the full armor of God. When we wear God's armor, we will be able to fight against the devil's evil tricks. We don't fight against people on earth. We are fighting against the rulers and authorities and powers of this world's darkness. We are fighting against spiritual powers of evil. That's why we need God's full armor. Then we will be able to stand strong against bad things. And when the fight is over, we will still be standing.

So stand strong, with the belt of truth tied around your waist. And on your chest wear the protection of right living. On your feet wear the Good News of peace to help you stand strong. Use the shield of faith to stop the burning arrows of the devil. Accept God's salvation as your helmet. And take the sword of the Spirit, which is the teaching of God. Pray in the Spirit at all times. Pray for everything you need. You must always be ready and never give up. Always pray for God's people.

Faith in Jesus
1 Peter 1:3–12

Give praises to the God and Father of our Lord Jesus Christ. God gave us great mercy and new life. Because Jesus rose from death, God gave us a living hope. We hope for the blessings that God has for his children. They are kept for us in heaven, and can't be destroyed or spoiled. God's power protects us because we have faith in him. He keeps us safe until our salvation comes.

Sometimes troubles come. They help to prove that we have faith. The purity of our faith is more precious than gold—it will bring us

praise and glory and honor when Jesus comes again. We haven't seen him and we still believe in him. Our faith has a goal—to save our souls. We are receiving that goal, our salvation.

The prophets tried to learn about this salvation. They had the Holy Spirit with them, telling them about the troubles and sufferings that would happen. They tried to learn about it all so they could understand. They were shown that their service was for you. They were preaching the Good News of Christ to help you know the truth.

King of Kings

*Revelation 21:1-4,
10-11, 22; 22:12*

Then I saw a new heaven and a new earth. The first heaven and the first earth had disappeared. Now there was no sea. And I saw the holy city coming down out of heaven from God.

I heard a loud voice from the throne that said, "Now God's home is with men. He will live with them, and they will be his people. God himself will be with them and will be their God. He will wipe away every tear from their eyes.

There will be no more death, sadness, crying, or pain. All the old ways are gone."

The angel carried me away to a very high mountain. He showed me the holy city, Jerusalem. It was coming down out of heaven from God. The city was shining with the glory of God! It was the most beautiful thing, sparkling and dazzling like an expensive jewel.

I did not see a temple in the holy city. The Lord God and the Lamb are the city's temple.

The city does not need the sun or moon to shine on it. The glory of the Lord is the city's light!

Then the angel of the Lord told me, "Listen! I am coming soon! I will bring rewards with me. I am the Alpha and the Omega, the First and the Last, the Beginning and the End."

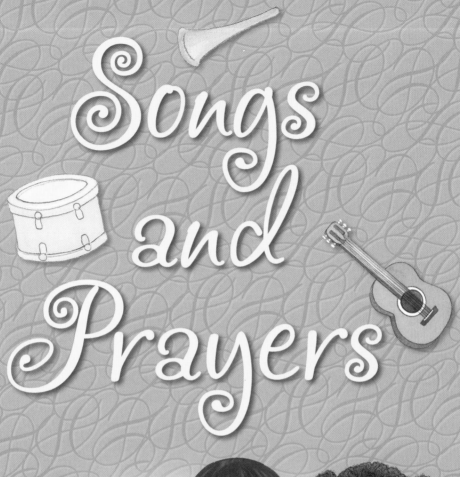

Songs and Prayers

The B-I-B-L-E

The B-I-B-L-E!

Yes, that's the Book for me.

I stand alone on the Word of God,

The B-I-B-L-E!

Jesus Loves the Little Children

Jesus loves the little children,

All the children of the world.

Red and yellow, black and white—

They are precious in his sight.

Jesus loves the little children
of the world.

Jesus Loves Me

Jesus loves me, this I know,

For the Bible tells me so;

Little ones to him belong,

They are weak, but he is strong.

Yes, Jesus loves me!

Yes, Jesus loves me!

Yes, Jesus loves me!

The Bible tells me so.

—Anna B. Warner

Amazing Grace

Amazing grace, how sweet the sound,

That saved a wretch like me!

I once was lost, but now am found,

Was blind but now I see.

—John Newton

Prayers

May the love of God our Father

Be in all our homes today;

May the love of the Lord Jesus

Keep our hearts and minds always;

May his loving Holy Spirit

Guide and bless the ones I love—

Father, mother, brothers, sisters,

Keep them safely in his love.

—Unknown

Thank you, Lord, for giving me

A happy, caring family.

Thank you for the friends I meet,

And for the neighbors down the street.

But most of all, dear Lord above,

I thank you for your precious love.

—*Unknown*

*L*ord, make me an instrument of
your peace.

Where there is hatred, let me sow love;

Where there is injury, pardon;

Where there is despair, hope;

Where there is darkness, light;

Where there is sadness, joy.

—St. Francis of Assisi

You made the sun to shine in the day,

The moon and stars to light up
the night.

You made the skies, the earth,
the seas.

Thank you, God, for all of these.

Amen.

Thank you, God, for my family.

Thank you for my friends.

Thank you, most of all, for Jesus.

And his love that never ends.

Amen.

God is great, and God is good.

Let us thank him for our food.

By his hand we all are fed;

Thank you, Lord, for our daily bread.

Now I lay me down to sleep.

I pray the Lord my soul to keep.

Your love be with me through the night

And wake me with the morning light.

—*Traditional*

A Prayer from Someone Who Loves Me . . .

_____

_____

_____

_____

_____

_____

_____

My Own Bedtime Prayer . . .